CROWN OF LOVE

STORY & ART BY **YUN KOUGA**

Table of Contents

Story Thus Far

Hisayoshi's hard work tutoring Rima pays off, and she passes Hakuo High's entrance exam. Hisayoshi is excited to be going to school with Rima, but juggling classes and work keeps
her usy—and keeps Hisayoshi from getting any closer.
Rim o w ried abo her mother who has vanished.
Mea in the rtainm ess,
a T to
air
Hi
bu

Rima Fujio

Hisayoshi "Kumi" Tajima

CROW
OF LOVE

You say you love me, but saying you love me doesn't do anything for me. Love by itself is not enough.

OKAY!
TAJIMA-KUN, IT'S A GO!
WE'RE GOING TO START LAYING DOWN THE TRACK!
GOOD WORK, EVERYONE!
SO, IKESHIBA-SAN, THIS SONG HAS A TIE-IN?
IT'S THE ENDING THEME FOR HIGH SCHOOL 1311.
OH THAT!
HUH? ARE YOU SERIOUS?!
I LOVE HIGH SCHOOL 1311!
EEK!
I HAD NO IDEA!
YEAH, IT WAS A LAST-MINUTE DECISION.
WHAT?
YOU'RE SUCH AN OLD FOGY, HISAYOSHI!
IT'S ON LATE ON THURSDAY NIGHTS! DON'T YOU WATCH IT?
THERE ARE ALL THESE NEW HOTTIES IN IT.
I DON'T KNOW AS MUCH ABOUT CELEBRITIES AS YOU DO, SHINGO.
YOU'RE SUCH AN OLD FOGY!
IF YOU CAN'T RECOGNIZE THE CELEBS, YOU'RE OVER THE HILL!

ANYWAY, SHOULD YOU EVEN BE WATCHING LATE-NIGHT TV?
HEH
I CAN'T REALLY CONDONE THAT KIND OF UNHEALTHY LIFESTYLE.
SIP
ACK!
SHOCK
ALL OF A SUDDEN YOU'RE TALKING LIKE KAZAMA-SAN!
DON'T TREAT ME LIKE A KID!
I MAY BE YOUNG, BUT I SLEEP DURING THE DAY, SO IT'S FINE!
ANYWAY, YOU HAVE TO WATCH THAT SHOW!
GRRRR
YOU SHOULD WATCH IT LATER ON VIDEO.
Uh-huh.
IF YOU DON'T SLEEP AT NIGHT, YOU'RE NEVER GONNA GROW ANY TALLER.
WHA?!
THAT WOULD BE A PROBLEM! I'M PLANNING TO GET A LOT BIGGER!
GRRR
I WANT TO BE AS TALL AS YOU, HISAYOSHI.
YOU BETTER SLEEP A TON THEN.

WHAT DID YOUR BODY SO MUCH GOOD?
I WASN'T PICKY. I ATE EVERYTHING. AND OF COURSE I DRANK MILK!
OH, RIMA!
YOU MUST BE HARD AT WORK TOO!
I SAW YOUR COM-MERCIAL.
YOU LOOKED REALLY GOOD.
OH YEAH?
TAJIMA-KUN, YOU ALWAYS SEEM SO RELAXED ABOUT IT ALL...
...BUT I'M NOT GOING TO LOSE.
THERE'S NO WAY I COULD OUTSHINE YOU, FUJIO-SAN.
WHY ?!
DON'T YOU WANT TO?

I'M THE LAST PERSON WHO SHOULD LECTURE SOMEONE, BUT...
GASP
SOB
I--
I'M SORRY, SHINGO-KUN.

HISA YOS ...
WHAT WAS SHE SO MAD ABOUT?
I REALLY DON'T LIKE IT WHEN GIRLS GET MAD AT ME.
YEAH.
YEAH ...
I MEAN ...
WINNING OR LOSING ...
OBVIOUSLY THAT'S IMPOSSIBLE.
I'll give you anything you want.
I'll do anything you want me to do.
What can I do to make you love me?

BEEEP

Minaho

Oh, those are drawing tools. Cuz I'm joining a painting club.

...

BEEP

WHAT HAPPENED?

I MEAN, ARE YOU DEPRESSED, KUMI-CHAN?

I'M TOTALLY DEPRESSED.

IKESHIBA
I FEEL LIKE I'VE FAILED SOMEHOW.
BEEP
LIKE RIMA JUST HATES ME EVEN MORE NOW.

I DON'T KNOW WHY, BUT I THINK RIMA HATES ME.
GLOOM
RIMA-CHAN? HATES YOU? UH-OH...
BEEP
DAD, DID YOU DO SOMETHING BAD AGAIN?
DAD DID NOTHING OF THE SORT.
I THINK HE'S JUST REALIZED...
...THAT GETTING PHYSICALLY CLOSE TO SOMEONE...
...DOESN'T ALWAYS MAKE YOU CLOSER EMOTIONALLY.

PHYSICALLY CLOSE?!
What's up with that?! Ack!
I JUST MEAN THAT THEY SEE EACH OTHER MORE NOW.
AND I DON'T THINK HISAYOSHI-KUN KNEW THIS, BUT...

INSIDE RIMA-CHAN IS AN INTENSELY COMPETITIVE ...
... GUY, YOU KNOW.
A GUY ?!
HE JUST MEANS IT'S A VERY MASCULINE QUALITY.
You shouldn't be so shocked.
AT ANY RATE, RIMA-CHAN ISN'T THINKING ABOUT ROMANCE RIGHT NOW.
A HARD PERSON TO FALL FOR.
Humph.
YEAH, BUT...
...IT WOULDN'T BE THIS HARD IF HE COULD JUST STOP LOVING HER LIKE THAT.
YOU'RE A GOOD KID, SHINGO-KUN.
THERE ARE A LOT OF PEOPLE WHO STOP LOVING SOMEONE BECAUSE IT'S TOO PAINFUL.

THAT'S NOT LOVE.

MAYBE NOT.

HERE'S A BLANKET.

OKAY, THANK YOU.
IF YOU WANT, I CAN SET UP A REAL FUTON FOR YOU. IT'S JUST OVER THERE.
THAT'S OKAY.
I WANT TO SLEEP WITH HISA-YOSHI.

ACK, YOU'RE STILL AT IT? THAT'S SO SAD!
BEEP
...

GOOD NIGHT, THEN.
SHINGO-KUN.

WOULD YOU GIVE UP ON THE PERSON YOU LOVED...
...EVEN IF IT GOT PAINFUL?
OF COURSE I WOULDN'T! A REAL MAN COULD NEVER DO THAT!
KUMI-CHAN, YOU TOO?
OBVIOUSLY, THAT'S WHY HE'S DEPRESSED.

HE WOULDN'T BE SO DEPRESSED IF HE COULD GIVE UP ON RIMA-CHAN.
SHINGO-KUN, DO YOU LIKE RIMA-CHAN?

I DO!
BUT I THINK HISAYOSHI'S BETTER FOR HER.
SO I DON'T MIND LETTING HIM HAVE HER.
I THINK YOU'D BE BETTER WITH SOMEONE YOUR OWN AGE THAN WITH SOMEONE OLDER.

SOME-ONE...
...THE SAME AGE?
YEAH.
GLEAM
HEY, HISA-YOSHI?
HMM ?

WHAT DO YOU THINK ABOUT A GIRL MY OWN AGE?
IT'D BE REALLY GOOD, DON'T YOU THINK?

I SEE. YOU AND RIMA-CHAN ARE THE SAME AGE TOO, RIGHT?
HMM ...

HEY, HISAYOSHI. AREN'T YOU GOING TO SLEEP?
MM, IN A LITTLE WHILE.
DIDN'T YOU SAY IT'S NOT GOOD TO STAY UP ALL NIGHT?
MM...

YURIE, WHAT ARE YOU WATCHING SO LATE?
IF YOU'RE WATCHING A VIDEO, LET ME WATCH TOO. WHAT IS IT?
EEEK!
HARU-KA?!
NO, DON'T COME IN! DON'T LOOK!
W-WHAT ?!

AKIRA, YOU LOOK SO CUTE IN THIS COMMERCIAL. AND THAT BOY IS ADORABLE.
I REALLY LIKE THIS ONE.
THANKS.
BUT YOU KNOW, YOU CAN'T SEE MY TRUE POTENTIAL IN A LITTLE COMMERCIAL LIKE THIS.

RING
CLICK
HELLO?
THIS IS TOKU-GAWA.
WHAT IS IT, IKESHIBA-SAN?
YAWN
WOULD YOU TAKE SOME PHOTOS OF HISAYOSHI-KUN FOR ME?
I WANT TO MAKE A PORTFOLIO.
HUH?
WHAT?
AWE-SOME! A PORTFOLIO OF HISA-YOSHI!
AND I'M IN CHARGE?
JOLT
YEAH, BUT NO NUDITY.

HUH? THAT'S A NO-NO?
THAT'S NO FUN! WHAT'S THE PROBLEM? IT'S NOT LIKE HE'S A WOMAN!
WELL, IF YOU REALLY WANT TO DO IT, I GUESS IT WOULD BE OKAY.
You want to take them?
WELL, MAYBE NOT NUDES, BUT I WANT ALL KINDS OF PHOTOS.

INCLUDING ONES OF HIM AT SCHOOL.
AT SCHOOL?!
I GET IT! LIKE A DAY IN THE LIFE... INTERESTING.

IF I'M TAKING PHOTOS OF HISA-YOSHI, THERE'S SOMETHING I WANT TO DO.
LEAVE IT ALL TO ME. IT WILL DEFINITELY BE INTER-ESTING.
OF COURSE.
THAT'S WHY I CALLED YOU.

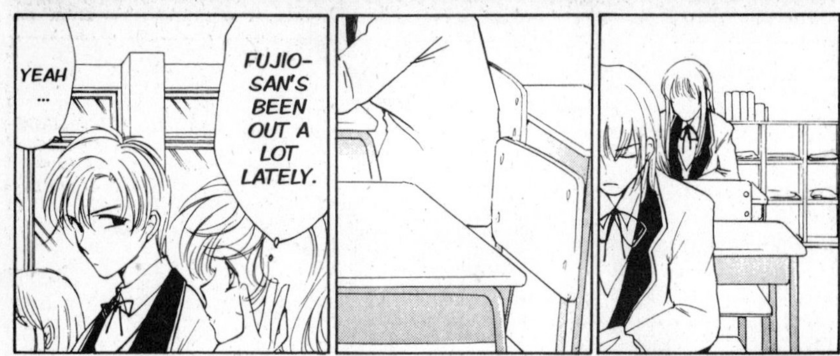
FUJIO-SAN'S BEEN OUT A LOT LATELY.
YEAH ...

Only ...
...when I see her, she just gets mad at me, but when I don't see her at all, I'm even...

...more of a wreck.

Am I getting greedy?

At first I never thought I'd get to meet her.
I was so wrapped up in following her, but even a picture made me happy.

But now...
I feel like I'm going to collapse just because I can't see her.

Maybe I'm asking too much.
No, but wait a sec...

If this is asking too much...

...then having her love me...

...is a total fantasy!
That won't work!

DING
DONG
HISA-YOSHI!
LUNCH! LET'S GO EAT!
THUNK

TOKU-GAWA! LONG TIME NO SEE!
It's been a while!
SORRY 'BOUT THAT!
I'VE BEEN BUSY WITH THE SCHOOL PAPER!
Heh.
OOH, IS THAT YOUR LUNCH?
MANA-CHAN MADE IT FOR ME.
LUCKY!
LET'S EAT IN THE CAFETERIA TOGETHER!
YACK
YACK
LET'S GO WITH LUNCH A!
OH, TOKU-GAWA-KUN! IT'S BEEN A WHILE!
I'LL GIVE YOU EXTRA!
THANKS!
I'LL TAKE YOUR PICTURE NEXT TIME! YOU'LL LOOK BEAUTIFUL!
HISA-YOSHI, LET ME TAKE YOUR PICTURE.

HMM ...

IT DOESN'T MATTER. I JUST WANT A PICTURE OF IT.

JUST ACT NATURAL.

SURE, BUT WHILE I'M EATING?

WHY DO YOU WANT A PICTURE OF THAT?

I'VE GOT A FEW PLANS MOVING FORWARD.

THINGS FEEL GOOD.

SO HOW IS HE?

HISA-YOSHI TAJIMA.

I SAW THE COMMERCIAL. VERY CINEMATIC.
HE DOES HAVE A VERY DRAMATIC AURA.
HE'S EXCITING TO WATCH.
EXCITING?
Hmm...
YES.
AND...
...HOW ARE THINGS WITH HIM AND RIMA FUJIO?

THERE'S NOTHING HAPPENING, SADLY.
IT WOULD BE A PROBLEM IF THERE WERE.
ALL JOKING ASIDE...

HE'S GOT GUTS, AND HE'S GOT A GOOD SENSE ABOUT THINGS. HE'S NO SHRINKING VIOLET.
AND HE'S VERY PROPER. HE WAS RAISED IN A GOOD FAMILY.
OH, IS THAT SO?

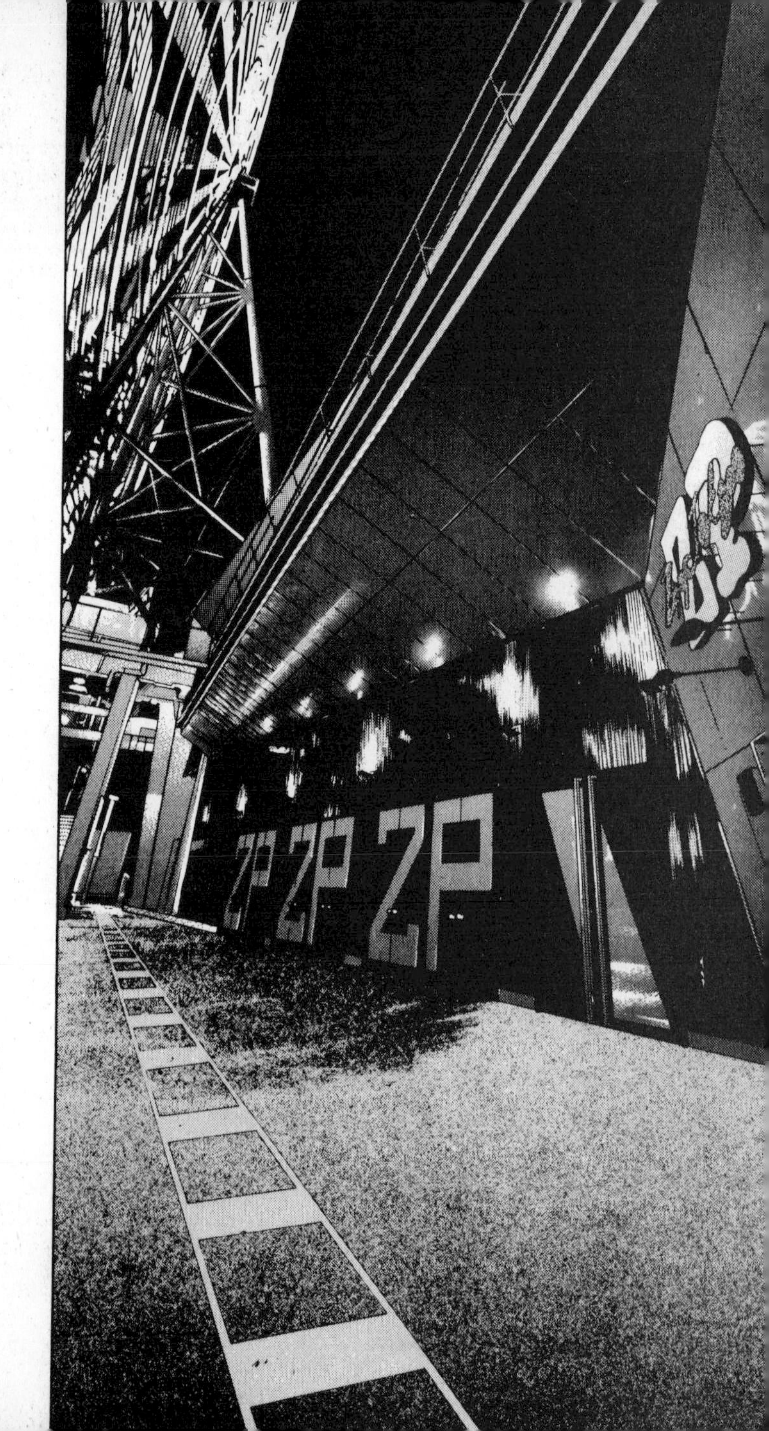
ZP
ZP
ZP

Lately I get the feeling she's totally avoiding me again.

NOTES?

THAT'S OKAY. I HAVE FRIENDS TO COPY NOTES FROM IF IT'S JUST A QUIZ.

THAT'S A GOOD THING!

WHAT'S THE USE OF YOUR LOOKING AFTER HER ALL THE TIME?

I MEAN, I UNDERSTAND YOU FEEL A LITTLE LONELY.

But how am I supposed to be helpful to her?

YOU SHOULDN'T FOLLOW ME TO WORK TOO MUCH.
IT'LL BE A PROBLEM FOR YOU TOO IF ANY WEIRD RUMORS GET STARTED.

It wouldn't be a problem.

But if things keep going like this, does that make me a stalker?

BUT RIMA IS AN ESTABLISHED CELEBRITY, AND IN SOME WAYS, WE CAN'T COMPETE WITH THAT.

AND BESIDES, YOU REALLY DON'T WANT TO BE "THE HELPFUL GUY," RIGHT?

DON'T YOU WANT HER TO FALL FOR YOU? GET A GRIP, HISAYOSHI.

OH WOW ...
WHAT HAPPENED TO KUMI-CHAN?
THIS IS REALLY BAD.

PAT
YOU'VE REALLY DROPPED THERE, TAJIMA-KUN— NO. 48!
AT THE RATE YOU'RE FALLING, YOU MAY NOT BE ABLE TO RISE UP AGAIN.
IT'S EASY TO GO DOWN, BUT COMING BACK UP ISN'T SO EASY.
BUT IF YOU'RE OUT, THEN I'LL GET A RECOMMENDATION, SO IT HELPS ME OUT!
Later!
WHAT THE HELL!
THAT PISSES ME OFF!
YOU SHOULD TELL HIM OFF!
KUMI-CHAN, DOESN'T THAT PISS YOU OFF?
SULK
NOT REALLY.

I DON'T CARE ABOUT MY RANKING.
Shut up.
Who cares about that?
OOH, SOME-ONE'S IN A PISSY MOOD!
KUMI-CHAN, YOU'RE SO CUTE!
TWITCH
IT'S TRUE.
TAJIMA-KUN REALLY IS CUTE.
HE CAN'T CONCENTRATE ON HIS STUDIES.
HIS HEAD'S SO FULL OF FUJIO-SAN.
IT SUCKS FOR YOU, YURIE.
IT'S OKAY.

AW, ALL ADULTS THINK OF IS LOVE AND ROMANCE.
BUT HE NEEDS TO STUDY NOW, OR HE'LL RUN OUT OF TIME.
I'M KIND OF DIS-APPOINTED IN KUMI-CHAN.

NOW ALL HE TALKS ABOUT IS FUJIO. SHE'S HOT, BUT STILL.
I DON'T REALLY CARE, BUT...
AT THIS POINT IT'S REALLY LAME.
I NEVER THOUGHT HIS GRADES WOULD GO DOWN LIKE THIS.

AWW, HE USED TO HAVE THAT ALOOF HANDSOME-NESS...
BUT NOW HE'S JUST LIKE ALL THOSE WEIRD FUJIO FANBOYS.
DON'T DIS TAJIMA-KUN!

YURIE, I GET HOW YOU FEEL, BUT WHY DON'T YOU GIVE IT UP?
KUMI-CHAN'S CHANGED.
DON'T LUMP ME IN WITH YOU GUYS. I'M SERIOUS ABOUT HIM.

YEAH, YOU THINK SO?

I MEAN, IF SOMEONE CHANGES, THEY BECOME A DIFFERENT PERSON.

I...

IF YOUR FEELINGS CHANGE JUST BECAUSE THE PERSON'S CHANGED...
...THEN THAT'S NOT REAL LOVE.

...BELIEVE IN TAJIMA-KUN. HE HASN'T CHANGED.
I DIDN'T FALL FOR HIM BECAUSE OF...
...HIS GRADES OR BECAUSE HE'S GOOD-LOOKING!!

...

YURIE, YOU'RE A TRUE ROMANTIC! YOU'VE GOT MY SUPPORT!
GLOMP
DON'T TEASE ME.

CAREER COUNSELING
THIS ISN'T GOOD.
FLP
WHY HAVE YOUR GRADES FALLEN SO DRASTICALLY?
YOU'VE BEEN A LITTLE RESTLESS LATELY.
HOW IS HE AT HOME?
Y— YES.
PLEASE EXCUSE ME. AT HOME HE HASN'T REALLY BEEN...
I'M SO SORRY.
WELL, NOTHING'S GOING TO HAPPEN RIGHT AWAY.
YES.
I REALLY DO APOLO-GIZE...
THUNK
THAT'S ENOUGH!
H-HISA-YOSHI?!
WHY DO YOU KEEP APOLOGIZING, MOM?!

THIS IS JUST AN ISSUE OF RANKING. IT HAS NOTHING TO DO WITH MY PARENTS.

YOU DON'T HAVE A PROBLEM AS LONG AS MY RANK GOES UP, RIGHT?

STOP IT, HISA-YOSHI.

I'LL MAKE A PROMISE.

I'LL GET IN THE TOP TEN NEXT TIME. THAT'LL FIX IT, RIGHT? QUIT GRIPING.

SO NAIVE.

NO MATTER HOW YOU TRY TO DEFY THEM, YOUR PARENTS ARE YOUR GUARDIANS.
YOU CAN'T EVEN WIPE YOUR OWN ASS BY YOURSELF YET!
IF YOU DON'T WANT YOUR PARENTS CALLED IN OR TO BE GRIPED AT, THEN DO WHAT YOU'RE SUPPOSED TO BE DOING...
...IN THE FIRST PLACE!

YOU MAY LEAVE!
HISA-YOSHI, HERE.
WHAT IS THIS? I DON'T NEED IT!
JUST TAKE IT.
SO YOU'RE NOT A BURDEN ON IKESHIBA-SAN.
WON'T YOU...
...COME BACK HOME?
I CAN'T GO BACK.

YOUR FATHER'S WORRIED TOO.
THAT'S NOT TRUE.
HE ONLY THINKS ABOUT HIMSELF.
HISA-YOSHI...
DON'T SPEAK ABOUT YOUR FATHER LIKE...
I'M SICK OF HIM TRYING TO ACT LIKE MY FATHER!
HISA-YOSHI!
HE'S A COMPLETE FAILURE AS A FATHER!
WHY ARE YOU ALWAYS APOLO-GIZING, MOM?
YOU DON'T KNOW, HISA-YOSHI...
...JUST HOW HAPPY YOUR FATHER WAS...
...ON THE DAY YOU WERE BORN.

MOM!

OBVI-
OUSLY
...
I CAN'T
REMEMBER
THAT!

THIS
SUCKS.
I
MADE
MY
MOTHER
CRY.
NOT
COOL.

THEY TOLD ME TO COME BACK TO THE OFFICE AT SIX, RIGHT?
. . .
I DON'T EVEN WANT TO SEE IKESHIBA'S FACE.
. . .
WHERE CAN I KILL SOME TIME?
HUH?
HUH?

OH NO, I DON'T REALLY KNOW.
I DON'T LISTEN TO MUSIC MUCH.
UMM ...
HMM...

OH! ♥ HEY, SWEETIE. CAN YOU DO ME A FAVOR?
Hee!
?!
ME?!
CAN YOU FIND A CD FOR ME?
I'M LOOKING FOR RIMA FUJIO'S ALBUM. ♥
FUJIO-SAN'S ?!
THAT'LL BE OVER THERE.
WOW, THANK YOU! YOU'RE SO HELPFUL!
I KNEW I SHOULD HAVE ASKED A YOUNG PERSON!
HERE.
THANK YOU, SWEETIE! ♥ I WAS SO LOST!
I WON'T GIVE IT TO YOU UNLESS YOU STOP CALLING ME SWEETIE.
FUME
SWEETIE'S A LITTLE MUCH. ARE YOU MAKING FUN OF ME?

OH DEAR! I'M SORRY! I DIDN'T MEAN ANYTHING BY IT.

OH NO! I WASN'T MAKING FUN OF YOU.

He's about my daughter's age.

Well ...

...he won't believe me.

THAT'LL BE 1,223 YEN.*

OH, THAT'S RIGHT!

IF YOU'VE GOT TIME, WANT TO GO ON A DATE? I'LL PAY TO THANK YOU FOR YOUR HELP.

*ABOUT $12

UH... I'VE GOT TIME, BUT...

IT'S SET THEN! I'M SO HAPPY.

I'LL PAY, BUT I DON'T HAVE MUCH MONEY, SO DON'T WORRY. WHAT WOULD YOU LIKE?

I'M MITSU-KO.

AND YOU ARE?

Her hands are dry...

HISAYOSHI...

...and warm.

WOW! HISAYOSHI, YOUR HANDS ARE SO BIG! YOU'RE LIKE AN AFGHAN HOUND!

THE BIGGER THE FRONT PAWS, THE BIGGER THE DOG WILL GROW!

EEK!

NAH, I DON'T REALLY WANT TO GROW ANY MORE.

YOU MUST BUMP YOUR HEAD ON DOOR-FRAMES.

SOME-TIMES.

HOW TALL ARE YOU?

PEEK

ABOUT FIVE FOOT ELEVEN.

HOW OLD ARE YOU?

SEVEN-TEEN.

WHAT ABOUT YOU, MITSUKO-SAN?
I'M A LITTLE OLDER, AND I'VE GOT A KID.
YOU'VE GOT A KID?!
Seriously ?!
I DO! A REALLY CUTE ONE!

I GET IT! YOUR KID ASKED YOU TO GET THAT CD!
BOY OR GIRL? AN ELEMENTARY SCHOOL STUDENT?
GO
IT'S MINE. ♥
MY DAUGHTER LOOKS A LITTLE LIKE RIMA FUJIO.
OH!
TAP
YOU DO!
MITSUKO-SAN, YOU LOOK LIKE RIMA.
SO I'M SURE YOUR DAUGHTER DOES TOO. LET ME MEET HER SOMETIME.
WHAT? HISAYOSHI, WOULD YOU RATHER HAVE MY DAUGHTER THAN ME?

OF COURSE NOT!
I LIKE PRETTY OLDER WOMEN.
THAT'S PERFECT!
ONLY ...
THE GIRL I LIKE... SHE ALSO LOOKS LIKE RIMA FUJIO.

AH!
DON'T LOOK AWAY! DON'T LET YOUR GUARD DOWN!
I'M PLAYING FOR KEEPS!

YOU 27 LOSSE
YOU
LOSE

SHOCK
I didn't win once.
...

HISA-YOSHI-KUN, ARE YOU BAD AT FIGHTING GAMES?

YOU'RE JUST TOO GOOD AT THEM, MITSUKO-SAN.
WELL, YEAH.
YAY!
GET ME A PRIZE FROM THE CRANE GAME THEN. I CAN'T DO IT.
YAHOO!

OOH, GET ME THAT TELE-PANDA THERE!
IT'S IN KIND OF A WEIRD PLACE...

OH!
OH!
OH!
OOH!
YOU'RE ALMOST THERE, HISAYOSHI-KUN!
MITSUKO-SAN, DON'T YELL IN SUCH A WEIRD WAY!

HEY, WANNA TAKE PRINT CLUB PHOTOS?
WHAT FOR?
AWW... BUY ME A DRINK THEN.
SULK
I THOUGHT YOU WERE GOING TO BUY ME SOMETHING.
BUT I'M THIRSTY.
THAT'S NOT A GOOD EXCUSE.
WHAT DO YOU WANT?
PEACH WATER. THE BIG ONE. IT'S THE SAME PRICE, SO IT'S A GOOD DEAL
CAN YOU DRINK ALL THAT?!
Peach Water
TEA
CLICK
I WOULD LOVE TO TAKE PRINT CLUB PHOTOS WITH MY DAUGHTER.
WHY DON'T YOU?
NO WAY. SHE'D NEVER TAKE ONE WITH ME.
HMM, YEAH, WELL...
I WOULDN'T TAKE ONE WITH MY PARENTS EITHER.

WHY NOT ?!
WHY WON'T YOU TAKE ONE WITH YOUR MOTHER ?!
BOO
I'VE NEVER THOUGHT ABOUT IT BEFORE.
BESIDES, I HATE MY PARENTS.
WHY DO YOU HATE THEM?!
WHAM
ACK!
YOU'RE SO MEAN!
I'D TAKE ONE IF MY MOM WERE LIKE YOU, MITSUKO-SAN.
NO, SHE HATES ME.
WHY ?
YOU'RE SO CUTE!
BECAUSE I'M NOT VERY MOTH-ERLY.
I'M STUPID, LAZY AND BOY CRAZY.
OH, WELL THEN...
YOU DON'T HAVE TO BELIEVE ME!
GRR

YOU WERE RUDE TO ME.
CHOMP
THANKS FOR THE FOOD.

BAM

IS IT A BAD THING TO BE GOOD AT FIGHTING GAMES?

Ended up paying
WHAT HAPPENED TO YOU PAYING?

DOES LIKING PACHINKO MEAN I'M NOT MOTHERLY?
WAS SHE LONELY WITHOUT A FATHER?

MY DAUGHTER AND I ARE ALWAYS FIGHTING.
IT'S JUST THAT SHE PISSES ME OFF. SHE'S SO INSOLENT.
AND SHE ACTS LIKE I'M A NUISANCE. AM I REALLY THAT EMBARRASSING?

SO I RAN AWAY! LET HER WORRY ABOUT ME!
NOT THAT I THINK SHE WILL.
MITSUKO-SAN, YOUR KID...
SHE'S 17! SHE'S AN ADULT!
Seventeen?! Just how old are you?!

I'M 34.
GRR
I can tell!
YOU WERE JUST WONDERING HOW OLD I AM, RIGHT? HOW RUDE!
YOU DON'T LOOK 34.
HEH HEH HEH. I'M DISCIPLINED.
IN WHAT?

THE REAL PROBLEM...

...IS THAT BOYS DON'T KNOW HOW OLD A WOMAN IS.

BY TALKING TO YOU, I'D THINK YOU WERE ABOUT 5.

HOW RUDE! BUY ME AN APPLE PIE TO MAKE UP FOR THAT!

HEY.

GO HOME AND PATCH THINGS UP WITH HER.

IMPOSSIBLE.

WE COULD NEVER PATCH THINGS UP.

SHE LOOKS DOWN ON ME.

I'M SURE THAT'S NOT TRUE.

YOU'RE A FAMILY. IT'S JUST THE TWO OF YOU, RIGHT?

YOU HATE HIM EVEN THOUGH YOU'RE FAMILY, RIGHT?

YOU LOOK DOWN ON HIM, DON'T YOU?

You don't know, Hisa-yoshi...
...just how happy your Father was...
...on the day you were born.

He was so happy.

FWUMP
AHH, I ALWAYS GET SO NERVOUS AT INTERVIEWS.
I NEVER KNOW WHAT TO SAY.

HERE'S SOME HOT COFFEE.
OOH.
THANKS, IKE-SHIBA-SAN.
SO.
HAVE YOU FOUND MITSUKO-SAN?

I'M DONE WITH THAT WOMAN!
I'M NOT WORRIED! I MEAN, HOW OLD DOES SHE THINK SHE IS?
Man, she pisses me off.
SHE'LL BE 35 THIS YEAR!

HEY. I WONDER ...

...HOW WE LOOK TO PEOPLE?

LIKE A MOTHER AND SON?

HOW COULD THAT BE?! THAT MAKES ME ANGRY!
A COUGAR AND HER BOY TOY?
IDIOT!
TEACHER AND STUDENT.
YEAH, THAT'S NOT BAD.
BUT...
THE REAL ANSWER IS "A MYSTERY."
HMM...
OH, IT'S SIX O'CLOCK!
I HAVE TO GO TO THE OFFICE.
HUH?
CAN I COME TOO?

HEY, THAT'S ...
ISN'T THAT HISAYOSHI TAJIMA?
WHO'S THAT AGAIN?
THE NEW KID FROM R MUSIC.
OOH, WE WON'T GET A STORY ON HIM YET.
BUT LET'S TAKE SOME PHOTOS ANYWAY. HE'S GOT A WOMAN WITH HIM.
CLICK

RIMA-SAN, YOU DON'T HAVE TO DO THAT!

HUH?

BUT I'M DONE FOR THE DAY, AND THERE'S NOTHING ELSE TO DO.

YOU HAVE PLANS, RIGHT?

NO REAL PLANS.

I WAS JUST THINKING I MIGHT DO SOME SHOPPING ON THE WAY HOME.

RIGHT?

I REALLY DON'T HAVE ANYTHING PLANNED MYSELF!

HAVE FUN! ♥

IS THAT SO?
EXCUSE US THEN.
I'll just be alone if I go home anyway.
I don't have any friends.
YOU KNOW, IKESHIBA-SAN, I MIGHT BE KINDA GOOD AT CLEANING.
MY PLACE IS SUPER CLEAN.
SINCE I DON'T HAVE ANY-THING ELSE TO DO.
GO TAKE A BATH AND MAKE SURE YOU PACK.
I AM DOING THOSE THINGS!
AND I'M SINGING TOO, LIKE I'M SUPPOSED TO.

DOES IT GET A LITTLE LONEL ON YOU OWN
AYBE YOU HOULD MOVE TO THE DORMS AFTER ALL.
NAH.
NICE TO MEET YOU, FUJIO-SAN! THIS IS SO OVER-WHELMING!
I'M A HUGE FAN!
YOU REALLY ARE CUTE!
Outwardly
I DON'T KNOW WHAT'S SO GREAT ABOUT HER.
On the inside
I MEAN, SURE SHE CAN SING, BUT STILL.
SHE PROBABLY HAS CONNEC-TIONS.
HEY! THANKS TO YOU, THEY PULLED ME OFF THE COVER!
But her feelings end up coming out.
COOL IT. THE SAME THING WILL HAPPEN TO HER EVENTUALLY.

SOME STUFF HAPPENED...

...AND I FEEL MORE COMFORTABLE ON MY OWN.

I'M... REALLY BAD...

IF I'VE GOT SOMEONE THERE, I BECOME DEPENDENT ON THEM.

I'D RATHER BE BY MYSELF.

IT'D BE SCARY IF I COULDN'T DO ANYTHING WITHOUT SOMEONE THERE.

HEY! DON'T CHANGE THE SUBJECT!
CLICK
GO HOME AND PATCH THINGS UP WITH YOUR DAUGHTER!
SULK
NO WAY! THAT'LL NEVER HAPPEN!
CLICK
WHY DON'T YOU STAY OUT OF OTHER PEOPLE'S BUSINESS?!
IT PISSES ME OFF WHEN YOU SAY IT LIKE THAT.
CLICK
WELL, I'M PISSED TOO.
FORGET IT. I'M GOING HOME.

MITSU-KO-SAN!

DON'T YOU REALLY WANT TO PATCH THINGS UP WITH YOUR MOM AND DAD?
DON'T PROJECT ALL THAT ONTO ME!
BA-BMP

HEY.
THIS IS A WEIRD FIGHT THEY'RE HAVING.
SOME-THING ABOUT HIS PARENTS? IT COULDN'T BE-

Marriage ?!
SHE DOES SEEM OLDER.
IT COULD BE...

GRP

HI! ♥ EVENING, HONEY.

DID YOU STRIKE OUT TONIGHT OR SOME-THING?
WANT TO GO SOME-WHERE AND HAVE SOME FUN WITH ME?
WHA?
WHAAT?

WHY DON'T I COME ALONG?
AHH!
COME ON NOW, MITSUKO-SAN.
I JUST LEFT YOU!
SORRY 'BOUT THAT.
BUT THIS ONE'S WITH ME.
JUST LEAVE ME ALONE!
AND DON'T CALL ME "THIS ONE"!
I DON'T WANNA LISTEN TO A KID LECTURING ME!
SCREECH

THEN WILL YOU PROMISE ME SOMETHING, HISAYOSHI-KUN?
IF I APOLOGIZE TO MY DAUGHTER, WILL YOU APOLOGIZE TO YOUR DAD?

I CAN'T DO THAT.
I TOTALLY REFUSE!

WHAT'S SO EMBAR-RASSING?

BUT...

EX-CEPT...

YOU MADE IT LIKE THAT, RIGHT, MITSUKO-SAN?

OH.

THAT'S ONE OF THE TWO BIGGEST TABOOS!

SAYING "YOU RAISED HER THAT WAY" OR "IT'S MY LIFE."

BECAUSE WHAT CAN I SAY TO THAT?

YEAH YEAH YEAH.

I'M VERY SORRY.

IT'S A REALLY TASTELESS THING TO DO! NOT TASTY!

ARE YOU HUN-GRY?

What're you talking about?!

SCREECH

HUH?

STARE
SHF
YOU IDIOT! DON'T USE THE FLASH!
IT WAS AN ACCIDENT!
YOU'RE NOT SOME AMATEUR. WHAT'RE YOU DOING?
FUME
I KNOW I'M CUTE ...
...BUT YOU CAN'T JUST GO TAKING PICTURES.
AND I'M IN A MAJOR BAD MOOD RIGHT NOW!
SHF SHF
NO!
HISA-YOSHI-KUN!
ACK! WAIT!
TAJIMA-KUN. VIOLENCE ISN'T—

RING-A-LING
IT'S ME.
IS THIS SOME SPY CAPER?
YES?
AT SHIBUYA POLICE STATION?
YES.
TA-JIMA-KUN IS...
GOT IT.
TAJIMA-KUN AND A WOMAN WERE TAKEN DOWN TO THE POLICE STATION.
WHAT?!

SHIBUYA POLIC
Lost
SAFE DRIVING WEEK
Police Wanted
STOP!
Stop drug use
Six o'clock... the office...
ZZZ
YOU'RE IN HIGH SCHOOL, AREN'T YOU?
YES.
I UNDER-STAND, BUT YOU NEED TO CALM DOWN A LITTLE.
YES.
SO YOU'RE A CELEBRITY? MUST BE TOUGH.
YES.

Aww, Ikeshiba's coming. Just another thing I owe him For. Damn.
ERK

EXCUSE ME. COULD WE BORROW A BLANKET?

SURE THING.

BA-BUMP

Oh.

UGH!
Rima too?! Why?!
Oh man, this sucks!
SHHK
...
M-M...
MOM?!

W–
WHY ARE YOU WITH TAJIMA-KUN?!

HUH?
BLINK

MO–
I'M MITSUKO FUJIO, AGE 34. WHAT A SURPRISE!
RIMA, YOU AND TAJIMA-KUN KNOW EACH OTHER?

YOU'RE SURPRISINGLY QUICK TO FIGHT, AREN'T YOU?
NO. UM...
No, I just hit him the tiniest bit, and he fell over...
AND WHERE HAVE YOU BEEN?!
TREMBLE TREMBLE

WHAT THE HECK? I WASN'T CAUSING ANYONE TROUBLE.
SULK
LET ME DO WHAT I WANT.

YOU'RE TOO OLD TO CAUSE PEOPLE SO MUCH TROUBLE LIKE THIS!
I CAN-NOT BELIEVE YOU!

OF COURSE I WILL.
I DON'T CARE, AND I DON'T WORRY ABOUT YOU EITHER.
I THOUGHT YOU WERE GONE, AND THERE YOU WERE FOOLING AROUND WITH STUPID TAJIMA-KUN.

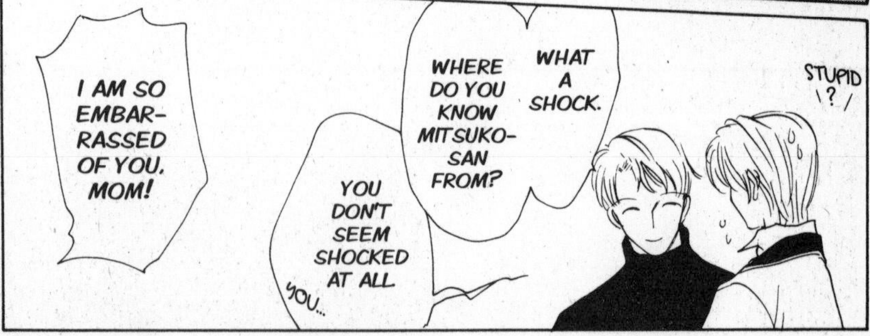
STUPID
?
WHAT A SHOCK.
WHERE DO YOU KNOW MITSUKO-SAN FROM?
YOU DON'T SEEM SHOCKED AT ALL.
YOU...
I AM SO EMBAR-RASSED OF YOU, MOM!

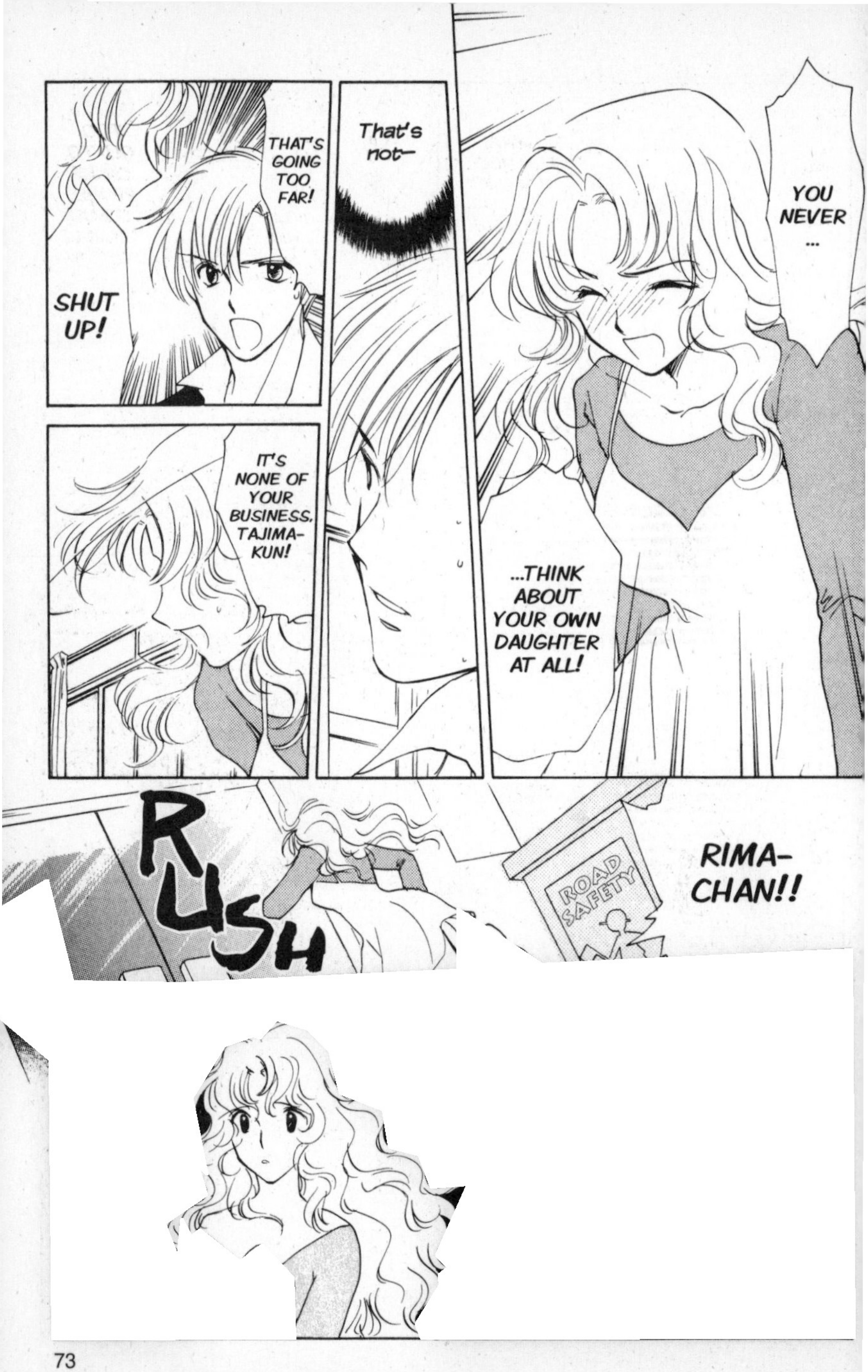

YOU NEVER ...

...THINK ABOUT YOUR OWN DAUGHTER AT ALL!

That's not—

THAT'S GOING TOO FAR!

SHUT UP!

IT'S NONE OF YOUR BUSINESS, TAJIMA-KUN!

RIMA-CHAN!!

RUSH

ROAD SAFETY

MITSU-KO-SAN!
ONCE I BRING RIMA BACK HERE...
DON'T CRY, MITSUKO-SAN.
SH-
SH-
SHE'S SO RUDE TO ME!
SOB SOB SOB
SHE GOT HER LOOKS FROM ME!
WHO DOES SHE THINK GAVE THEM TO HER?
you didn't literally give them.

SNIFF

I CAN'T DO IT!

WHY DOES SHE HATE ME SO MUCH ?!

WAAAAAH!

PAT

MI-TSUKO-SAN.

I'LL BRING HER BACK.

I'LL BRING HER BACK.

DON'T WORRY!

OFF I GO.

Hisayoshi-kun.

LET'S LEAVE THIS TO HISAYOSHI-KUN.

GUH

UH

UH

UH

THANK YOU, IKESHIBA-SAN.
YOU'RE SO NICE.
RIMA'S SUCH AN IDIOT.
HONK
YOU'RE MARRIED, RIGHT?
SHE'S GOT THE SAME TYPE AS I DO, AND THE SAME DESTINY.
MITSU-KO-SAN.
SNFF
IKESHIBA-SAN, YOU LOOK A LOT LIKE RIMA'S FATHER.
HE WAS MY HIGH SCHOOL TEACHER, AND HE WAS MARRIED WITH CHILDREN.
I KNEW FROM THE BEGINNING THAT I COULDN'T MARRY HIM.
BUT...
WHAT'S THAT GOT TO DO WITH ANYTHING?

THIS IS MY PUNISHMENT FOR FALLING IN LOVE WITH SOMEONE ELSE'S HUSBAND.
FOR RIMA TO HATE ME SO MUCH!

YOU THINK SO?
I THINK THAT YOU AND SHE ARE QUITE ALIKE.
STRONG WILLED, PASSIONATE, LONELY...
...AND STUBBORN.

AND THE REASON RIMA'S ANGRY WITH YOU IS BECAUSE YOU DID SOMETHING WRONG.
It's not some punishment.
HONK
OH DEAR.

SHE'S JUST OBSESSING OVER ME AS A SUBSTITUTE FOR A FAMILY. IT'S NOT LOVE.

I'M NOT ...
...RIMA-CHAN'S DESTINY.
WAIT!
LET GO OF ME!
I KNOW YOU WERE WORRIED!
I WASN'T!
WHAT ARE YOU TALKING ABOUT?
AND ANYWAY, WHY WOULD SHE...
IT'S JUST THE TWO OF US, BUT I GUESS THIS MEANS I'M THE ONLY ONE WHO THINKS THAT WAY!

THAT'S NOT TRUE.
I KNOW THAT'S NOT TRUE.
WHA-
Ooh, I'm gonna cry!
WHAT THE HECK?
YOU DON'T KNOW ANYTHING, TAJIMA-KUN.
IF I WERE YOUR MOTHER ...
...I'D NEVER LET A DAUGHTER AS CUTE AS YOU GO.
WHAT ARE YOU TALKING ABOUT?
SOB
AT LEAST SAY IF YOU WERE MY FATHER.

DON'T YOU FEEL BAD FOR MAKING YOUR MOTHER CRY?
HMPH
AS IF SHE'D CRY!
URK☆
YOU TWO REALLY ARE RELATED.

AND HOW DO YOU KNOW MY MOM ANYWAY?

UH, YOU SEE... I MET HER IN THE CITY AND SORT OF HELPED HER OUT.

I DON'T REALLY GET IT.

SO WHY DO YOU KEEP TAKING MY MOM'S SIDE?

IF YOU KEEP BABYING HER, SHE'LL JUST TAKE ADVANTAGE OF IT!

WHY ARE YOU BEING SO NICE TO HER?!

BECAUSE...

...SHE'S YOUR MOTHER.

YOURS.

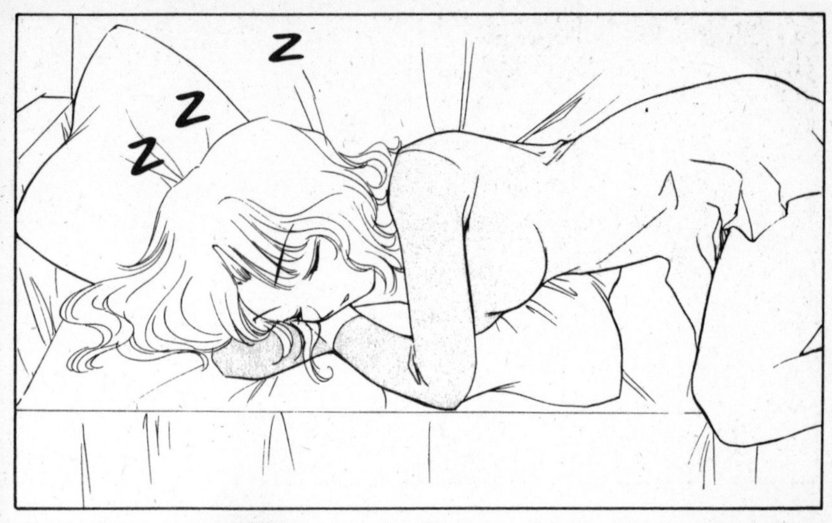
Z
Z
Z

OH.
URGH
OH GOOD, RIMA-CHAN.
I'VE BEEN NEEDING TO USE THE REST-ROOM.

I-
IKE-SHIBA-SAN.
LOOK AFTER MITSUKO-SAN.
I CAN'T BELIEVE THIS! SHE'S AN ADULT.
WAKE UP!
...

SO. THINGS ARE ALL SETTLED WITH THE ASSAULT.

HUH?

Assault? You mean me?

BE CAREFUL NEXT TIME.

BUT TO THINK YOU KNOW MITSUKO-SAN.

YOU ALWAYS SURPRISE ME.

I'M KIND OF SCREWED.

GUESS I NEED TO GET OFF MY HIGH HORSE NOW.

I'M GOING TO SETTLE THINGS WITH MY FATHER.

I REALIZED THAT I CAN'T BE HIS EQUAL IF I'M RUNNING AWAY.

SIGH
URGH! I REALLY DON'T WANT TO.
PAT
OH.
MITSUKO-SAN TOLD ME SOMETHING GOOD.

RIMA-CHAN IS HEREDITARILY DISPOSED TO LIKE INTELLIGENT GUYS.

What's hereditarily?

SERIOUSLY? THAT MEANS...

...I MIGHT HAVE A CHANCE?

OH YEAH.

CLACK

...

CLICK

...

HERE WE ARE.
WOW... YOU LIVE IN A NICE PLACE.
HEY. DON'T TALK SO LOUDLY.
THE OFFICE RENTS THIS PLACE FOR ME.

BUT IT REALLY IS A NICE PLACE.
WOW.
IT'S OKAY.
OOH, YOU'RE SO IMPU-DENT!
URGH
It's okay, she says!
HEY, YOU KNOW WHAT?
FLUP
DID I USED TO SAY I WANTED MY OWN PLACE?
I DON'T REALLY...
...CARE ABOUT...
...ALL THAT.
I DON'T REALLY CARE WHERE I LIVE.
FOR ME...
MY HOUSE IS...

BLUSH
NEVER MIND!

FWP
FWP

WHAT IS IT?
I'M ASKING SERIOUSLY FOR ONCE.
IT DOESN'T MATTER! I'M GOING TO BED. I HAVE TO GET UP EARLY TO-MORROW.
YOU CAN FIT IN MY PAJAMAS, RIGHT?

THEY MIGHT BE A LITTLE TIGHT IN THE CHEST.
Hee hee
IDIOT. NO THEY WON'T.
THEY MIGHT BE A LITTLE TIGHT IN THE STOMACH AND BUTT THOUGH.
What an awful thing to say!
I CAN MAKE DO, BUT...
...WHEN I WAKE UP, LET'S GO SHOPPING FOR THINGS FOR ME.

HUH?
HUH?
WHAT DO YOU MEAN, "HUH?"
YOU'RE NOT GONNA BUY ME ANYTHING? I DON'T HAVE ANY MONEY.

YOU-
YOU'RE GOING TO STAY HERE FOREVER?
I-
I-
I'M STAY-ING.
I'M GOING TO STAY. IS THAT BAD?
BAD? MOM...
I WORKED HARD RAISING YOU, SO NOW I GET TO LIVE OFF OF YOU.
WHAT'S WRONG WITH THAT? IT'S MY RIGHT AS A MOTHER.

THERE'S NO RIGHT LIKE THAT!
WHAT?
I CAN'T?!
SOB
SOB

...
BUT YOU HAVE TO DO HALF THE HOUSE-WORK!

CLICK
GOOD NIGHT ...
... THEN.
WHAT ARE YOU DOING?
DON'T YOU HAVE YOUR OWN BED?
IT—
IT'S FINE. I'M GOING TO SLEEP HERE TONIGHT.
MAYBE I'LL USE THE BED THEN.
NO!
YOU HAVE TO SLEEP HERE.

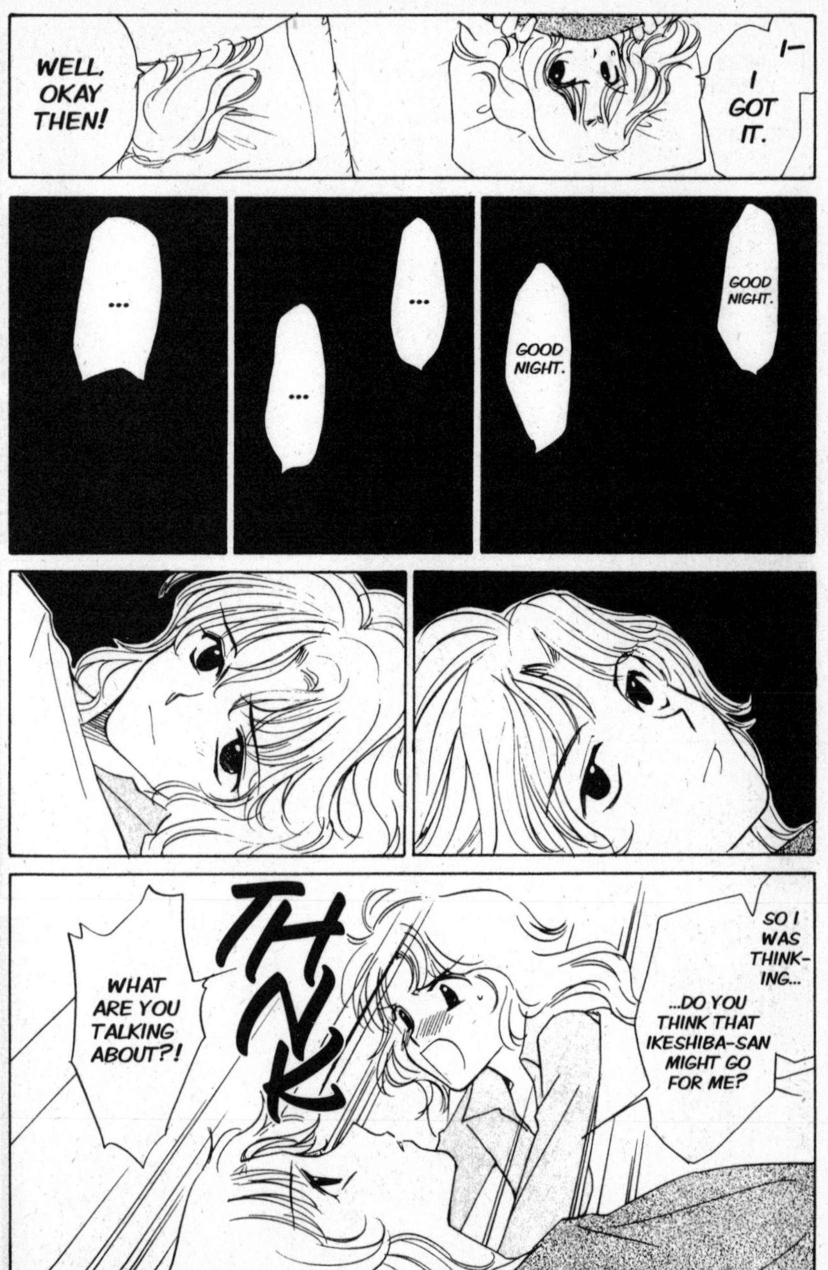

I— I GOT IT.
WELL, OKAY THEN!
GOOD NIGHT.
GOOD NIGHT.
...
...
...
SO I WAS THINKING...
...DO YOU THINK THAT IKESHIBA-SAN MIGHT GO FOR ME?
THNK
WHAT ARE YOU TALKING ABOUT?!

THERE'S NO WAY A CHILD COULD EVER LAND A MAN LIKE HIM.

YOU'RE TOO OLD, MOM!

I DON'T THINK HE'D BE AGAINST A WOMAN LIKE ME.

I CANNOT BELIEVE YOU!

MOM, YOU'RE SO SHAME-LESS!

BUT I DON'T MIND DISAPPEAR-ING.

IF YOU THINK I'M IN YOUR WAY, THEN...
...I'LL DIS-APPEAR.
DIS-APPEARING IS ALL I'M GOOD AT.

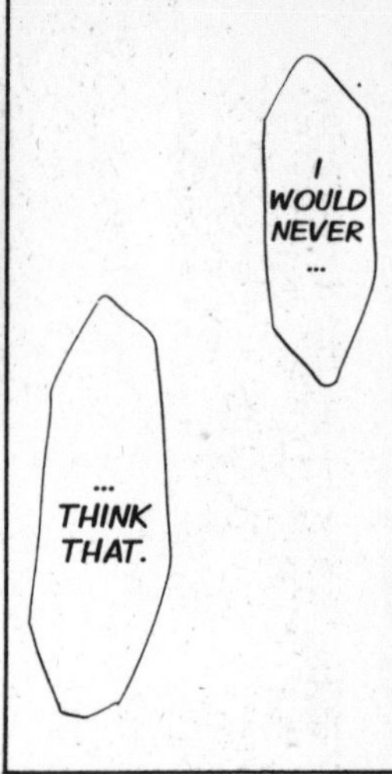

I WOULD NEVER ...
... THINK THAT.

...

HEY, DON'T FALL ASLEEP ON ME!
SNORE
She sleeps just as easily as ever.

IDIOT.

That's right.

The two of us are both terrible.

We hate being alone.

But because we won't settle for just anybody, we always end up alone.

GRP

DING DONG
OH.
I WONDER WHO IT COULD BE SO LATE.

WHO IS IT?
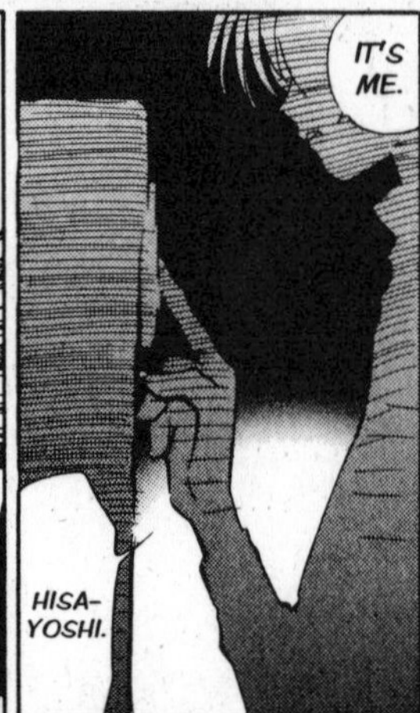
IT'S ME.
HISA-YOSHI.

CLICK
HISA-YOSHI?!
WHAT IS IT? DID SOME-THING HAPPEN?

GOOD EVEN-ING.
WELCOME HOME! COME IN.
YOU CAME BACK!

DEAR...
HISA-YOSHI CAME HOME.
OH.
YOU THINK YOU CAN JUST WALTZ BACK IN HERE AFTER THE WAY YOU SPOKE TO ME?

I HAVEN'T REALLY COME BACK...
...SIR.

WHAT IS IT?

COME INSIDE.

NO, I'M NOT COMING IN.

I DECIDED I'M NOT COMING HOME FOR A WHILE.

HISA-YOSHI?!

SO WHAT DID YOU COME HERE FOR?

TO ASK YOU TO FORGIVE ME.

I WANT TO REACH MY POTENTIAL.

I'VE FOUND WHAT I WANT TO DO.

SO PLEASE LET ME DO THAT AS LONG AS I WANT TO.

BUZZ
DON'T ACT LIKE SUCH A SPOILED BRAT!
SLAM
I'M NOT ACTING LIKE THAT...
YOU IDIOT.
STOP IT, BOTH OF YOU.
YOU'RE BOTHERING THE NEIGHBORS. COME NSIDE.
... SIR.
NO, I WON'T COME IN.
NOT UNTIL HE FORGIVES ME.
YOU THINK YOU'RE GOING TO GET YOUR WAY?
I DO!
I MEAN, YOU'RE ON MY SIDE, RIGHT?

PARENTS HAVE TO BE ON THEIR KID'S SIDE.

NOT BE THEIR ENEMIES!

SO I WANT YOU TO UNDER-STAND ME!

YOU LOVE ME, RIGHT?
I'M SPECIAL TO YOU, RIGHT?
YOU ALWAYS PUT ME FIRST, RIGHT?

UP UNTIL NOW...

GRP

I THOUGHT IT DIDN'T MATTER IF YOU UNDERSTOOD ME.

I THOUGHT YOU NEVER COULD!

BUT I CAN'T DO THAT ANYMORE.

I WANT YOU TO UNDER-STAND ME.
AND I WANT YOU TO FORGIVE ME.
IF I CAN'T MAKE MY ALLIES UNDERSTAND, THEN WHAT CAN I DO?

YES, SIR.

I CAN'T KEEP UP WITH YOU.
TSK
WHERE DID YOU LEARN TO SWEET-TALK PEOPLE LIKE THAT?
DEAR!

MONEY.
YE— YES?
STARE
YOU COME BARREL-ING IN HERE LIKE A HEAD-ON COLLI-SION.
THAT KIND OF APPROACH IS COWARDLY.
COME ON.

WE'RE GOING DRINKING.
CLICK
YOU GO ON TO BED.

MY, BUT THAT TAJIMA BOY...

...HISA-YOSHI HAS GOTTEN HAND-SOME!

HE ALWAYS WAS HANDSOME.

SPEAKING OF WHICH, I HEARD HE'S GOING TO MAKE HIS DEBUT OR SOME SUCH.

WEL-COME.
WHY, TAJIMA-SAN!
OOH, SO THERE WILL BE TWO OF YOU TODAY?

THIS IS MY SON.

HEY.

HE'S CUTE! ♥

JUST LIKE TAJIMA-SAN.

HERE'S A HOT TOWEL.

THANKS.

I'VE NEVER BEEN...

...TO A PLACE LIKE THIS BEFORE.

IT'S NO BIG DEAL. YOU'RE WITH YOUR GUARDIAN.
RUB
RUB
?

YOU'RE ...
... TALL, AREN'T YOU?

YEAH. SO ARE YOU.

DAD.
YOU'LL BE HAVING WHISKEY AND WATER, RIGHT? ♥
OF COURSE.
IT'S IN MY GENES.

DRINK.
OLD
DLETON
HISKEY

I CAN DRINK ALCOHOL FINE.
THEN DRINK.

SIP

SIP
YEAH ...
THAT'S ALSO MY GENES.
...
GULP
YOU LOOK LIKE YOU CAN HOLD YOUR LIQUOR WELL.
YEAH.
WAIT A MINUTE.
LOOKS LIKE THEY'LL BE ON TO BOTTLE TWO SOON.
OH DEAR, THAT TAJIMA-SAN...
I HOPE HIS SON WILL BE ALL RIGHT.
KLINK
YOUR MOTHER ...

...HAS ALWAYS HAD THE WRONG IDEA BECAUSE SHE'S A SIMPLE WOMAN.
I'M FOND OF HER. IT'S GODDAMN IRRITATING.
IF I WASN'T, WHY WOULD I GO AND MARRY SOMEONE LIKE HER?

HEY, DARLING ...
LET'S NAME HIM HISAYOSHI.
I WANT TO USE A CHARACTER FROM YOUR NAME.
HE'S OUR TREA-SURE.

THERE WERE A THOUSAND MORE ATTRACTIVE WOMEN.

SWAY
I DON'T ...
...THINK THAT'S RIGHT.

HMPH
THE WOMEN YOU LOVE AND THE WOMEN YOU'RE ATTRACTED TO ARE TWO DIFFERENT THINGS.
YOU THINK SO?
YOU THINK SO? I DON'T THINK SO.
TWAP
DON'T YOU FALL IN LOVE WITH HER BECAUSE YOU'RE ATTRACTED TO HER?!
Shut it.
BRAT.

NO. DON'T BOTHER.
WELL THEN, WHAT WILL YOU DO? YOU CAN'T CARRY HIM HOME.

IKESHIBA HOME

COME ON NOW, HISA-YOSHI-KUN.
ARE YOU ALL RIGHT?
MM...

I HAVE AN IDEA.

AND THAT'S WHY I FELL FOR HER, SO...
HELLO? I APOLOGIZE FOR CALLING SO LATE.

HE WON'T THINK OF ANYTHING BUT GOING BACK TO YOUR HOUSE.
APPARENTLY HE'S MADE UP HIS MIND HE'S NOT GOING HOME.

THANK YOU, TAJIMA-SAN.
I REALLY DON'T KNOW.
IS GIVING HIM HIS FREEDOM...
...ANDONING HIM OR RUSTING HIM?

I THINK THAT'S ...
...UP TO HISAYOSHI-KUN.
I don't get it.
When in the world...
THAT'S TRUE ...
CER-TAINLY ...
...did he become an adult?
GRADUATION CEREMONY
BUT I CAN STILL DRINK HIM UNDER THE TABLE.

WAIT, RIMA.
W-W-WAIT!
TAKE THIS!

I'M OFF!
EEK. I'M CUTTING IT CLOSE!
SH

TAKE THIS WITH YOU. I MADE IT FOR YOU!
HAVE A GOOD DAY.
G
R
P
THANKS.
I'M OFF...

ARE YOU SURE IT'S OKAY?
THIS LUNCH ...
HOW RUDE! I'M VERY CONFIDENT IN IT! VERY!
SQUEAK
I MADE IT.
GET ON, FUJIO-SAN!
TA-JIMA-KUN!
C'MON.
NO NEED TO HOLD BACK!
I—
I'M NOT. AFTER ALL, I'M RUNNING REALLY LATE.
THUD
THAT'S GOOD.
NO IT'S NOT!

PUT YOUR ARMS AROUND ME. IT'S DANGEROUS.
HUH?
HOLD ON TIGHT.
OH...
Wait, grab on to him? Where?
OKAY.
WHAT IS IT?
N-NOTHING.
I'm putting way too much thought into this...

THUNK
GOOD MORNING!
MORN-ING!
JUST UNDER THE WIRE!
BARE-LY.
TAJIMA-KUN, THAT WAS RISKY.
DING
DONG
HA HA
SLEEPY?
I WAS ON A RADIO SHOW UNTIL LATE.
I'M ABOUT TO FALL ASLEEP DURING CLASS.
THUNK
THAT WAS THE BELL, PEOPLE.

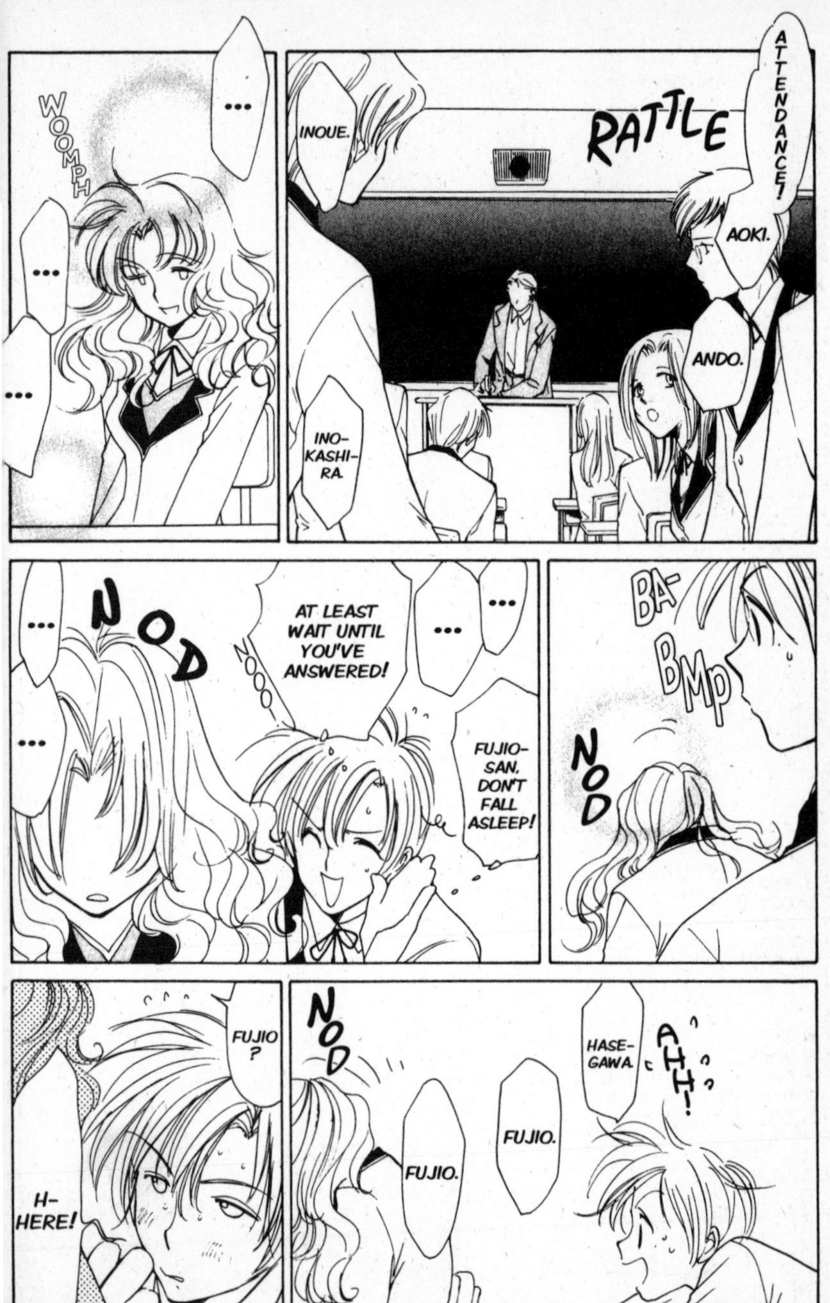

ATTENDANCE!
RATTLE
AOKI.
ANDO.
INOUE.
INO-KASHI-RA.
WOOMPH
...
...
...
BA-BUMP
NOD
...
...
FUJIO-SAN, DON'T FALL ASLEEP!
AT LEAST WAIT UNTIL YOU'VE ANSWERED!
NOOOO-
NOD
...
...
HASE-GAWA.
AHH!
FUJIO.
FUJIO.
NOD
FUJIO?
H-HERE!

DON'T MAKE WEIRD NOISES LIKE THAT.
YES, OF COURSE.

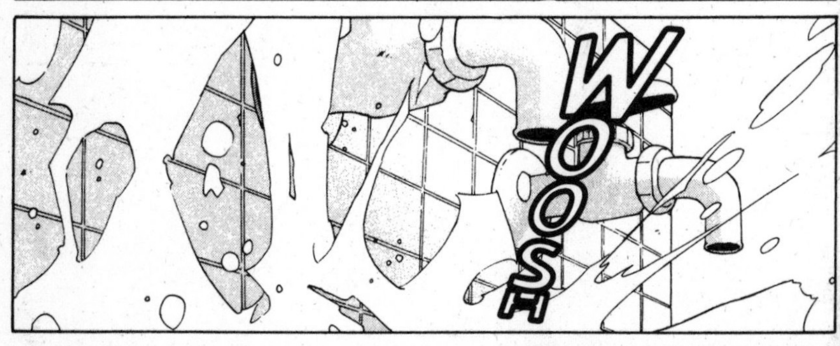
WOOOSH

OOOH. I WAS COM-PLETELY ASLEEP!
I SLEPT UNTIL LUNCH!
HERE'S A TOWEL.
THANKS, AKIRA-CHAN.
SCRUB
YOU BROUGHT LUNCH TODAY, RIGHT?
WANT TO EAT IN THE CAFE-TERIA? I'VE GOT TEA.

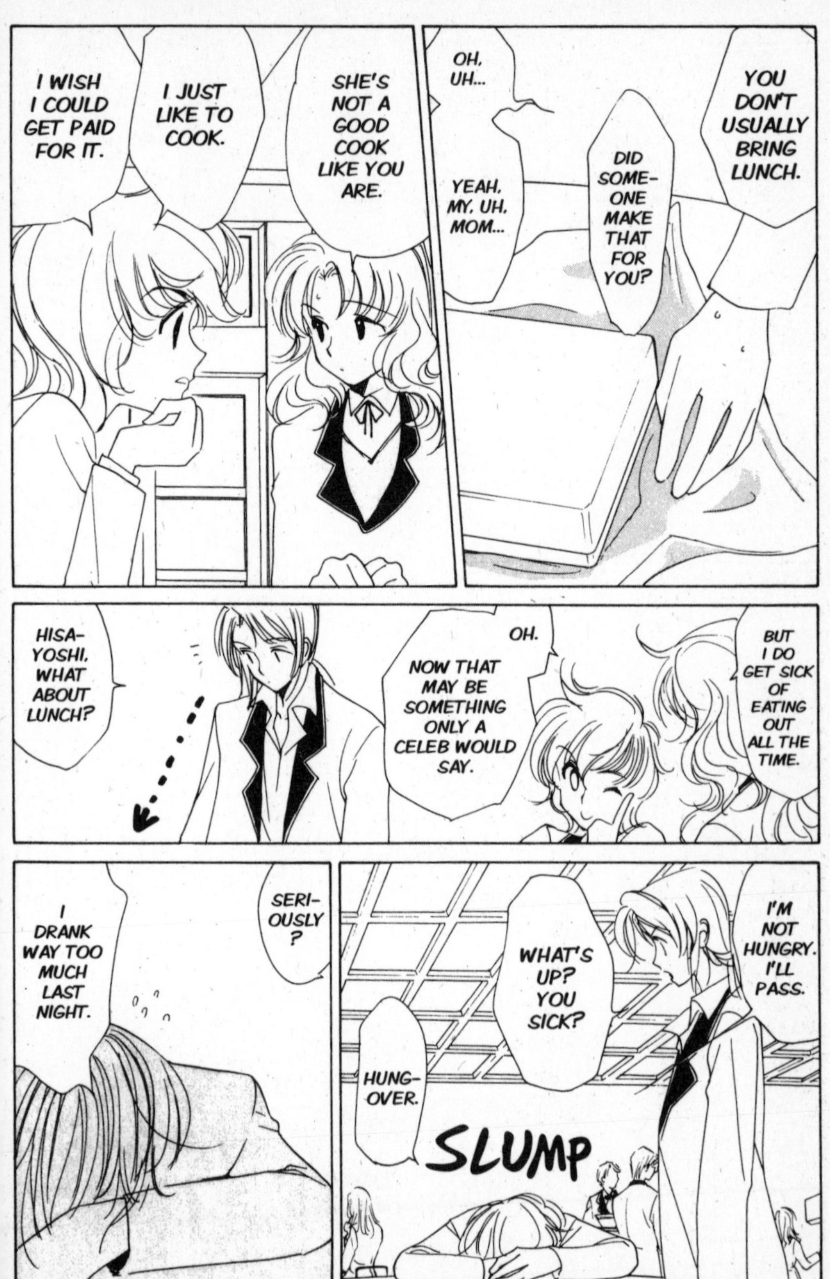
YOU DON'T USUALLY BRING LUNCH.
DID SOMEONE MAKE THAT FOR YOU?
OH, UH...
YEAH, MY, UH, MOM...
SHE'S NOT A GOOD COOK LIKE YOU ARE.
I JUST LIKE TO COOK.
I WISH I COULD GET PAID FOR IT.
BUT I DO GET SICK OF EATING OUT ALL THE TIME.
OH.
NOW THAT MAY BE SOMETHING ONLY A CELEB WOULD SAY.
HISA-YOSHI, WHAT ABOUT LUNCH?
I'M NOT HUNGRY. I'LL PASS.
WHAT'S UP? YOU SICK?
HUNG-OVER.
SLUMP
SERI-OUSLY?
I DRANK WAY TOO MUCH LAST NIGHT.

YOU IDIOT!
THAT'S SO DUMB, TAJIMA-KUN. DON'T OVERDO IT.
FUJIO-SAN...
AND WHAT ARE YOU DOING RIDING YOUR BIKE WITH ME FIRST THING THIS MORNING IF YOU FEEL LIKE THAT?
I APPRECIATE IT...
...BECAUSE THANKS TO YOU I GOT HERE ON TIME, BUT STILL.
WELL, I'M...
...GLAD THEN.

AFTER ALL, RIMA-CHAN, MEN LIVE FOR A WOMAN'S THANKS.
OOH ...
DON'T YOU MEAN FOR THE GIRL THEY LOVE?

YEAH WELL, I LOVE ALL GIRLS.
OH?! THAT'S A DEAL BREAKER FOR ME.
ME TOO.
ME TOO.
AND THEY ALL MAKE A BREAK FOR IT!

YOU'RE ALL SO MEAN!
WELL, ANYWAY ...
...THANKS FOR THIS MORNING.
ALSO, IT'S NOT GOOD FOR YOU TO DRINK TOO MUCH.

YEAH.

THANKS.

BLUSH

OH!

ACK, WHAT IS THAT?!

YOU'RE RIGHT! THAT'S SO WEIRD!

HUH?!

IT'S MORE THAN WEIRD, IT'S KIND OF UNBELIEV-ABLE.

THIS IS...

EEEEK

DID... MITSUKO-SAN MAKE THAT?

EVEN I COULDN'T MAKE THIS!

WAAAH!

The one thing I can do well is boil eggs.

Hee hee

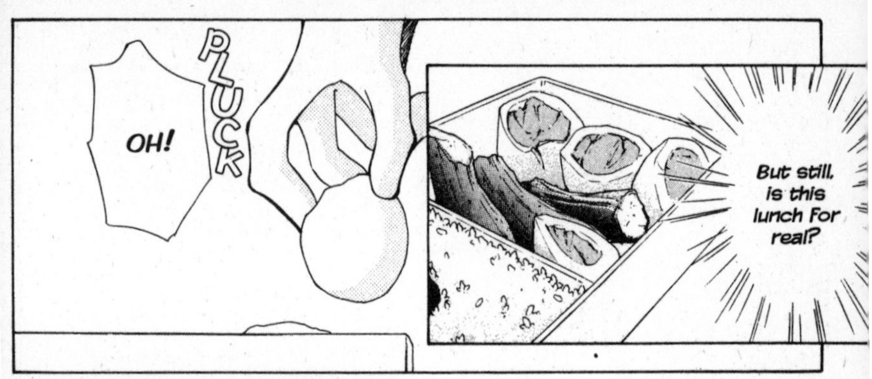

But still, is this lunch for real?
PLUCK
OH!

MUNCH
IT'S GOOD.
AREN'T YOU GOING TO EAT?
SULLEN
I'M GOING TO!

I CAN EAT THIS, AS LONG AS I THINK OF IT AS A BOILED-EGG DIET...

GULP

IT'S NOT SO BAD.

THEY'RE GOOD.

IS HOW THEY TASTE THE ISSUE HERE?

...

OH... UM...
UM, HEY, TAJIMA-KUN.
TAKE-ZAWA-SAN.
ARE YOU FREE THIS SUNDAY?
SOME OF US ARE TALKING ABOUT HANGING OUT.
COME ON, KUMI-CHAN!

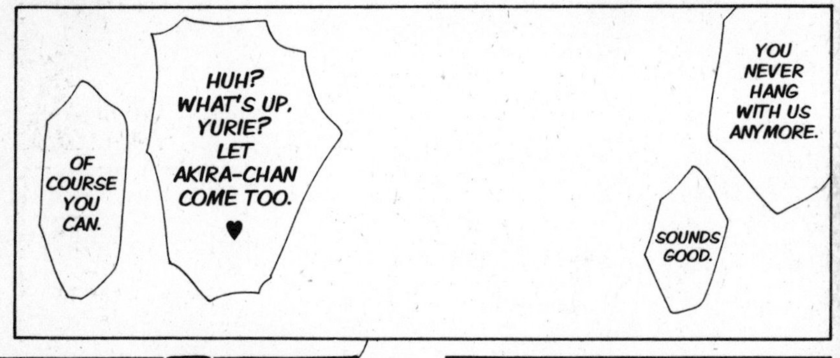

YOU NEVER HANG WITH US ANYMORE.
SOUNDS GOOD.
HUH? WHAT'S UP, YURIE? LET AKIRA-CHAN COME TOO. ♥
OF COURSE YOU CAN.

THEN CAN RIMA-CHAN COME TOO?
ME?!
THAT'S OKAY.
I DON'T NEED TO!
FWIP
FWIP
OF COURSE.
IF SHE WANTS TO.

IF YOU WANT TO...
...WHY DON'T YOU COME HANG OUT WITH US THIS SUNDAY?
AWW...
TNK
WHY'D YOU HAVE TO GO AND INVITE FUJIO-SAN, YURIE?
WE JUST WANT KUMI-CHAN THERE.
WELL, I GUESS I'M OKAY WITH IT IF YOU ARE, YURIE.
I THOUGHT TAJIMA-KUN WOULDN'T COME BY HIMSELF.
AND BESIDES...
IF WE LEAVE FUJIO-SAN OUT, IT'S LIKE WE'RE PICKING ON HER.
AND I WANT HIM TO REALLY FALL FOR ME...
...NOT JUST BECAUSE FUJIO-SAN ISN'T THERE.

I'M HAPPY I GET TO HANG OUT WITH HIM ON SUNDAY.

IF I WERE HIM, I'D GO OUT WITH YOU, YURIE!

SIGH

IT'S NOT GOING SO WELL, HUH?

HMM...
RIMA
FUJI
HANGING OUT WITH KIDS FROM CLASS?
IS THAT OKAY? THERE WILL BE A LOT OF GIRLS.
Y— YEAH.
IT'S FINE, BUT JUST DON'T DO ANYTHING THAT DRAWS TOO MUCH ATTENTION.
YOU NEVER KNOW WHO MIGHT BE WATCHING.
OKAY.

SO YOU MADE FRIENDS AT SCHOOL
NO, THEY'RE NOT REALLY FRIENDS...
THEY KIND OF JUST INVITED ME ALONG AS AN AFTERTHOUGHT.
IT'S TIME, FUJIO-SAN.
LET'S DO A GOOD JOB!
OKAY!
WE'RE ROLLING.
PLEASE COME OUT IN THE ORDER WE DISCUSSED.
OKAY! LONG TIME NO SEE, RIMA-CHAN.
NANAMI-CHAN.
HOW'VE YOU BEEN?
NOT BAD.
ARE YOU REALLY GOING TO SCHOOL?
WHENEVER I CAN.
WOW. WHO'D HAVE THOUGHT YOU'D HAVE THE TIME?
I'D HATE TO GO TO SCHOOL.

I MEAN, WE'RE CELEBRITIES. WHY WOULD YOU WANT TO GO TO SCHOOL?
THAT'S KIND OF WEIRD, FUJIO-SAN.
YOU THINK SO?
OH YEAH.
I MEAN, I HATE STUDY ING.
AND IT'S REALLY JUST A DETOUR, RIGHT?
HERE WE GO!
YOU'D BE BETTER OFF TAKING VOCAL LESSONS.
YOU KNOW?

AND OUR GUESTS FOR TODAY!
NA-NAMI!
OOOOOH
SEVEN SISTERS!

AND...
RIMA FUJIO!
SHE'S SO CUTE IN PERSON!
EEEK!
SO CUTE! ♥
SHE'S PRETTY SMALL, HUH?
EEEK!
DID SHE LOSE SOME WEIGHT?
THAT DRESS IS SO CUTE! ♥

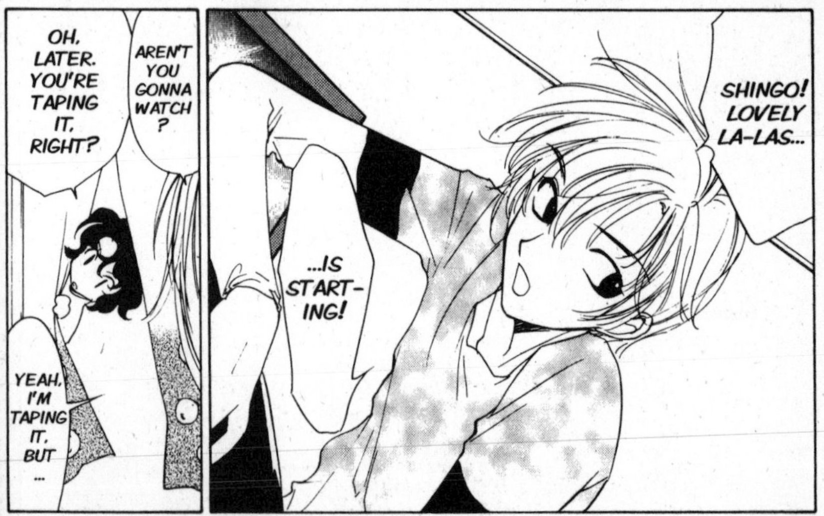

SHINGO! LOVELY LA-LAS...
...IS START-ING!
AREN'T YOU GONNA WATCH?
OH, LATER. YOU'RE TAPING IT, RIGHT?
YEAH, I'M TAPING IT, BUT ...

OF COURSE SHE DOES!
FLUTTER
RIMA LOOKS REALLY CUTE!
HMM ...
I SEE...
MUST BE NICE...
...TO BE YOUNG!

HEY, HEY!
MANA-CHAN...

WHAT, KUMI-CHAN?
ARE YOU FREE THIS SUNDAY?
I'M HANGING OUT WITH SOME FRIENDS. WANNA COME WITH?

WHAT'S WITH THAT?
WHAT ABOUT ME?
WHA!
YOU TOO, SHINGO, OF COURSE.
BUT YOU WANT ME TO INVITE MANA-CHAN, RIGHT?

YEAH, WELL...
ME?
C'MON, YOU SHOULD COME.

RIMA'S GOING TO GO TOO.
FOR REAL?
FOR REAL.

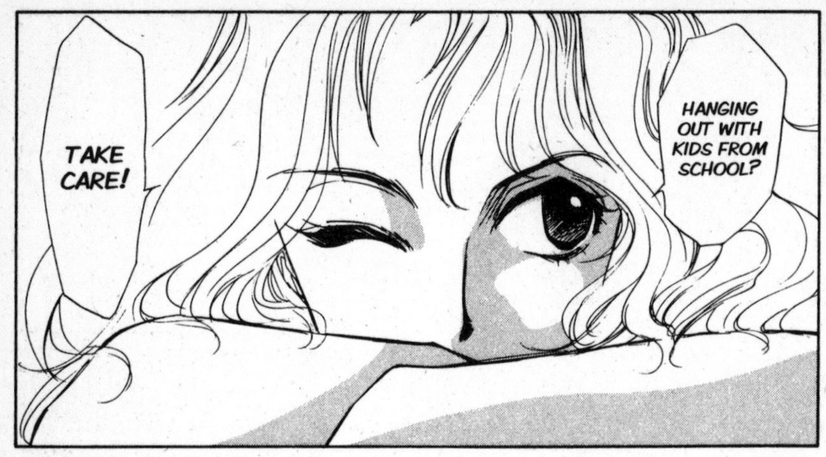
HANGING OUT WITH KIDS FROM SCHOOL?
TAKE CARE!

I RE-CORDED THAT SHOW FOR YOU.
THANKS.
BUT FRIENDS, HUH?
YOU'VE GOT FRIENDS.
I GUESS.

I NEVER HAD MANY GIRL-FRIENDS.
I LIKE GUY FRIENDS BETTER.
I NEVER GOT ALONG WITH THEM. THEY WERE ALWAYS SO CLINGY.

AND THAT'S YOUR PROBLEM.
WHAT IS?
YOU WANNA GO?!

2 26
I'M SO GLAD THE WEATHER'S NICE!
THIS PLACE GETS SO CROWDED ON SUNDAYS!

YOU'RE SO CUTE! ♥
ARE YOU KUMI-CHAN'S LITTLE BROTHER?
OR HIS LOVE CHILD?
YOU GIRLS REALLY LOVE THAT KIND OF THING, DON'T YOU?

THERE'RE SO MANY PEOPLE.
SO WE DON'T GET LOST.

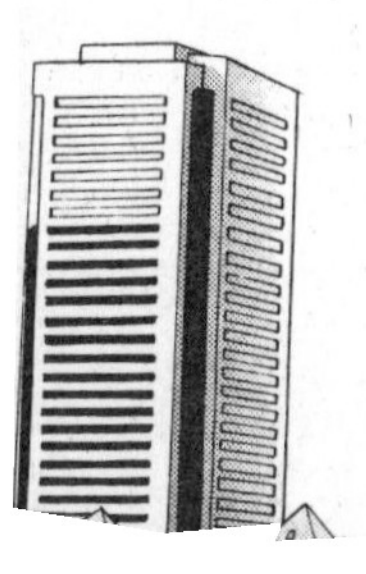

OOH, HOW CUTE!
PHOTO OP!
EEK!
JUST SHUT UP! I'LL PULL YOUR SKIRT DOWN!

FUJIO-SAN, YOU'RE TAKING PHOTOS?
THIS?
IT'S MY FAVORITE OF ALL THE DISPOSABLE CAMERAS.
IT TAKES PRETTY GOOD PHOTOS.

CAN I TAKE A PICTURE TOO?
BA-BMP BA-BMP
BA-BMP

IS THAT OKAY?
ARE YOU ALLOWED TO TAKE PHOTOS WITH EVERYONE?
YEAH.
IT'S FINE. DON'T WORRY ABOUT IT.

?

WELL THEN, LET'S START OFF WITH THE MOST PROBLEMATIC PHOTO!
A PIC OF JUST THE TWO OF US!
GRAB
AHH!

BUT...
You know...

I FINALLY GET TO TAKE A PHOTO WITH HER!

IDIOT.

MANA, YOU COME IN TOO.

NO FAIR, HISA-YOSHI!

LET ME IN TOO! ME TOO!

NO WAY!

LET'S TAKE ONE ALL TOGETH-ER.

Heh heh heh

IS THAT OKAY?

YEAH.

IT'S NO FUN BY MYSELF.

CLICK

AS LONG AS YOU GIRLS DON'T SELL THEM TO SOME MAGAZINE.
WE'D NEVER DO THAT!
WHAT A BRAT!
CLICK

WHAT SHOULD WE GO ON FIRST?
A ROLLER-COASTER.
HUH? MIDGETS CAN'T RIDE ON THOSE.
EEK
EEK
WHAT ?!
MIDGET ?!
YOU CAN RIDE ON THEM AS LONG AS YOU'RE 3'9"! I'M NOT A MIDGET!

CLICK

CLICK

MAN, I'M TIRED!
KUMI-CHAN, ICE CREAM!
WHAT?!
YOU'RE THE ONLY GUY, SO YOU NEED TO GO BUY IT FOR US!
OKAY!
I'LL GO TOO!
I'm a guy!
FUJIO-SAN, ARE YOU OKAY?
YEAH, I'M FINE, TAKE-ZAWA-SAN.
BUT I THINK I'M GETTING SUNBURNED. HA HA.
THAT MUST BE TOUGH.
HAVING A JOB AT YOUR AGE.
NAH.
I DO IT BECAUSE I LOVE IT.
THANKS FOR TODAY.
I HAD...
...A LOT OF FUN.

NO PROBLEM.
I WANTED TO KNOW WHAT YOU WERE LIKE ANYWAY.
WE DON'T HAVE MUCH CHANCE TO TALK AT SCHOOL.

I THOUGHT YOU WERE BEING UNFAIR...

...SINCE YOU KNEW HOW TAJIMA-KUN FELT ABOUT YOU...

NOT GIVING HIM A STRAIGHT ANSWER.

HUH?
NO.
NO, BUT... DO YOU THINK SO?
I THINK I DID TELL HIM. BUT... I GUESS WE'RE FRIENDS NOW.

THAT'S WHAT'S UNFAIR.

YOU'RE NOT FRIENDS.
IF YOU REALLY LOVE SOME-ONE...
...YOU CAN'T BE FRIENDS WITH THEM.

BA-BMP BA-BMP BA-BMP

YOU JUST PRETEND TO BE FRIENDS, AND YOU WAIT.
TAJIMA-KUN AND I, WE'RE BOTH JUST WAITING FOR OUR CHANCE.

I CAN'T HELP LOVING TAJIMA-KUN.
I WON'T LET YOU HAVE HIM, FUJIO-SAN.

TAKE-ZAWA-SAN...
YOU DON'T NEED TO WORRY ABOUT THAT.
MY JOB IS THE MOST IMPORTANT THING TO ME.
SO I DON'T MIND GIVING UP SCHOOL AND FRIENDS AND A BOYFRIEND FOR MY JOB.
I CAN'T HAVE IT ALL, SO I HAVE A LIST OF MY PRIORITIES.
AND MY JOB IS NUMBER ONE.
SO I DON'T NEED TAJIMA-KUN.

I THINK... HE'S A REALLY NICE GUY, BUT...

I'M NEVER GOING TO FALL FOR HIM.

HISA-YOSHI!

SHH.

RIIMAA, THAT'S CRUEL.
IT REALLY IS.
A NICE GUY, HUH?

YIKES

HISA-YOSHI!

HANG ON!

RIMA DOESN'T KNOW WHAT SHE'S TALKING ABOUT!

YEAH ...

YEAH.

THAT'S RIGHT! HISAYOSHI, YOU'RE SO HANDSOME, AND YOUR LEGS ARE SO LONG!

YOU'RE SO NICE! YOU'RE A REALLY GOOD PERSON! I DON'T KNOW WHAT MORE SHE COULD WANT!

...

I DON'T THINK IT'S A QUESTION OF THE KIND OF PERSON I AM.
I'M NOT EVEN ON HER RADAR TO BEGIN WITH.
AAAAAA-AAAAAA-AAAH!

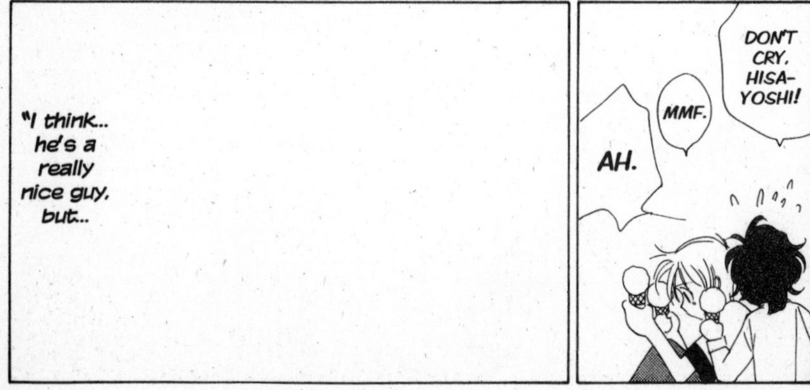

DON'T CRY, HISA-YOSHI!
MMF.
AH.
"I think... he's a really nice guy, but...

ONCE SHE CAL YOU A N GUY...
...IT'S PRETTY MUCH...
"... going to Fall For him."
... OVER.
...A BAD BOY THEN.
HERE'S YOUR ICE CREAM!
YAY! ♡
THANKS, KUMI-CHAN!
I DIDN'T BUY THEM FOR YOU GUYS! YOU EACH OWE ME 270 YEN!
HUH?
DON'T GIVE ME THAT!

I love you more than
anyone in the world.
It's an easy thing to think
and also an easy thing to say...
...but it's difficult
to get across...

...and even harder to make someone believe it.

OOH.

THE VIEW FROM THIS SPOT HAS CHANGED SO MUCH IN THE LAST FEW YEARS.

I GUESS.

WHAT'S UP, HISAYOSHI? YOU HAVE NO ENERGY. GET AHOLD OF YOURSELF.

NOTHING GOOD WILL COME OF YOU SPACING OUT LIKE THAT.

I GUESS.

I THINK I MIGHT BE...

...DE-PRESSED.

COMFORT ME. ♥

IDIOT.

DON'T ASK AN ELEMENTARY SCHOOL KID TO BABY YOU.

AND YOU'RE SKIPPING SCHOOL RIGHT NOW, AREN'T YOU?

OBVIOUSLY. SECOND PERIOD'S STARTING RIGHT ABOUT NOW.

DING
DONG
SHHK
SIGH
To Yurie
Kumi-chan's playing hooky! Wonder why? And Rima-chan's absent too. (Of course she's probably working.)

Dear Akira,
I don't think he's playing hooky. He's probably just not feeling well. I hope he gets better.
PLONK
SKRITCH SKRITCH
I'm positive he's not playing hooky! Tajima-kun's not that kind of person! If he's not coming in, there's got to be a reason for it.
AARGH
Whatre you talking about? He's playing hooky for sure! Now what if they were on a date?

Hello, Yurie-san?
That's called skipping
(You're saying you can just
stay home from school as long
as you've got a reason to?)
...
...
Some days are like that.
PLONK
HEY, HISA-YOSHI ... THIS PLACE ...
HMM?
SQUIRM
IT'S FULL OF COUPLES, ISN'T IT?

THEY'RE PRETTY SHAME-LESS, HUH?
SMOOCH SMOOCH
ICK.
I FEEL EMBARRASSED JUST WATCHING THEM. IT MAKES ME FEEL SO HOT AND STUFFY!

LUCKY THEM.
ARE YOU SERIOUS, HISAYOSHI ?!
YOU WANT TO DO THAT STUFF TOO?

YEAH.

BA-BMP
YOU KNOW, HISA-YOSHI...
...YOU MAY BE THE TYPE OF GUY THAT'S A TOTAL DEAL BREAKER FOR RIMA.

NO. I'M SORRY.
THAT'S NOT TRUE.
...
I CERTAINLY...
...CAN'T IMAGINE RIMA LETTING ME DO THAT STUFF.
NOOO!
DON'T TRY TO IMAGINE IT!
UM.
EXCUSE ME.
DO YOU HAVE A MINUTE?
IT'S JUST AFTER TEN.
YOU DUMMY! THAT'S...
THWAP
"DO YOU HAVE THE TIME?"

DO YOU HAVE A MINUTE?

NO.

NO? HISA-YOSHI...

POKE

YOU'VE GOT ALL THE TIME IN THE WORLD. YOU'RE SKIPPING.

YOU'RE SKIPPING SCHOOL?

NO.

WELL, KIND OF.

GRAB

THEN COME WITH ME!

I'LL PAY!

I MAY HAVE TIME...

...BUT THAT DOESN'T GIVE ME A REASON TO GO WITH YOU.

YOU DON'T WANT TO?

HOW SELFISH!

SELF-ISH?
HEY, HISA-YOSHI...
...THIS LADY'S KIND OF CRAZY.
Eeee!
HEE HEE HEE. YOU JUST FIGURED THAT OUT?
THAT'S RIGHT, I AM CRAZY.
YOU CAN'T RUN, SO YOU HAVE TO COME WITH ME.
HISA-YOSHI...
WAAAAAH
I'm scared.
THERE, THERE.
IF YOU DO WHAT I SAY, I WON'T KILL YOU.
FIRST, WE'RE RIDING ON THAT!

WHOA, IT'S SO HIGH UP...
I BET IT'D BE SCARY IF YOU STOPPED AT THE TOP.
WHACK
WHY ARE YOU SITTING THERE ?!
YOU'RE SUPPOSED TO SIT HERE! HERE!
WHACK
Oh man...
...

YOU'RE ...
...IN LOVE WITH SOMEONE, RIGHT?
AND IT'S UNREQUITED.

HEE HEE
HOW COULD I TELL?
WELL, YOU HAVEN'T EVEN ASKED MY NAME.
YOU'RE NOT INTERESTED, RIGHT?

GUYS ARE SO STUPID.
THEY CHEAT ON THEIR GIRLFRIENDS WHEN THEY HAVE THEM.
BA-BMP
BA-BUMP
I'm scared.
AND WHEN THEY'RE IGNORED, THEY GET PISSED OFF. IT'S SO STUPID.

ARE ALL THE GUYS YOU KNOW LIKE THAT?
BLUSH
WHAT. WAS I OFF?
YOU DON'T HAVE A GIRL-FRIEND, RIGHT?
EEP
EVERY-THING YOU SAID WAS RIGHT. BUT WHAT ARE YOU ANGRY ABOUT?
WHAT HAP-PENED?
I FEEL BAD FOR YOU BECAUSE YOU'RE SO BEAUTIFUL.
GULP

TO PUT IT POETICALLY...
MY LOVE AFFAIR HAS COME TO AN END.

LADY, YOU GOT DUMPED
SHINGO!!
THAT'S RIGHT! EXCUSE ME!

BUT MINE HAD A BEGINNING A MIDDLE AND AN END.

SO IT'S MUCH BETTER THAN YOUR AFFAIR, WHICH NEVER EVEN STARTED.

YOU'RE SCARED, AREN'T YOU?

YOU'RE SCARED TO TELL HER HOW YOU FEEL AND HAVE HER SHOOT YOU DOWN.
SO YOU DO NOTHING, LIKE A COWARD!
THAT'S NOT TRUE! HISA-YOSHI HAS...
...TOLD HER SO MANY TIMES AND GOTTEN TURNED DOWN SO MANY TIMES THAT HE'S EXHAUSTED NOW!
...
RAWR
IT'S TRUE THAT I'VE TOLD HER MANY TIMES AND SHE'S TURNED ME DOWN ALL THOSE TIMES, AND I'M EXHAUSTED NOW, BUT...
KOFF
...I'M JUST TAKING A BREAK RIGHT NOW. I HAVEN'T GIVEN UP.
THAT'S SO LAME!
HEE HEE
HAAA
You told her many times and she turned you down every time.
YOU THINK SO?
ACCORDING TO YOUR THEORY, WOULDN'T T BE MORE LAME NOT TO DO ANYTHING?

PAUSE
WHAT'S UNCOOL ABOUT BEING DUMPED?
IT'S NOT AT ALL LAME.
...
THAT'S TRUE.
IT'S NOT LAME AT ALL.

OOOH, LOOK AT THAT CUTE CHINESE DRESS! ♥
DON'T YOU THINK THAT'D LOOK GREAT ON ME?
IT WOULD. DO YOU WANT IT?
WANT ME TO BUY IT FOR YOU?
OOH, WELL THANKS, SWEETIE.
WHEN YOU GROW UP, RIGHT?
HEH HEH
HEY!
DON'T UNDER-ESTIMATE ME! I'VE GOT A LOT OF MONEY!

HEH. IS THAT SO?
GRR
IT'S YOUR DADDY'S MONEY, RIGHT? A MAN SHOULD SPEND MONEY HE EARNS.

HISA-YOSHI!
WAAAH.
ANYWAY, WHO'S HUNGRY?
There, there.
OKAY, WANT TO GO FOR CHINESE FOOD?
A PORK BUN?!
LET'S WALK.
HUH?!
IT'S FUN TO WALK AROUND THIS AREA.
And they've got shark-fin buns too.

THERE'S SOMETHING ELSE YOU REALLY WANT TO TALK ABOUT...
...ISN'T THERE?
MAYBE...
BUT THAT'S ALL...
THAT'S WHY YOU CAME UP...
...TO ME.

"Do you have a minute?"

SORRY. IT'S JUST THAT YOU LOOKED SO SERIOUS...
...I HAD TO MAKE A JOKE ABOUT IT.

I'll take five.
THAT'S SO MEAN!
Yes, ma'am!
Three pork and two shark fin.
Shark fin! Shark fin!

YOU'RE ACTUALLY PRETTY POPULAR, AREN'T YOU?
I MEAN, YOU'RE SO GOOD-LOOKING.
BUT I GOT DUMPED.

NO MAN WHO GETS DUMPED ALL THE TIME...
...COULD EVER SAY THAT GETTING DUMPED WASN'T LAME.
FWSH
BUT I DON'T ACTUALLY WANT TO GET DUMPED...
Seriously.

I WENT UP TO YOU BECAUSE YOU'RE SO GOOD-LOOKING.
BECAUSE THE GUY THAT I WAS IN LOVE WITH WAS THE GREATEST GUY IN THE WORLD...
...SO I FIGURED IF I NEEDED A REPLACEMENT, HE SHOULD AT LEAST BE HANDSOME.
YOU STILL LOVE HIM?
I DO.
BUT IT'S ALL OVER NOW.
YOU'RE GIVING UP EVEN THOUGH YOU LOVE HIM?
WHAT ELSE CAN I DO?
I CAN'T SEE HIM.
I CAN...
...NEVER...
...SEE HIM AGAIN.
SO DOES LOVE END WHEN YOU STOP SEEING THE PERSON?
CAN YOU QUIT JUST LIKE THAT?
I WISH I COULD DO THAT.

HE DIED YESTER-DAY.
THERE'S NO POINT IN CONTINUING TO LOVE HIM.

YOU'RE KIND OF...
...CRAZY.
MOST PEOPLE DON'T REACT LIKE THAT.

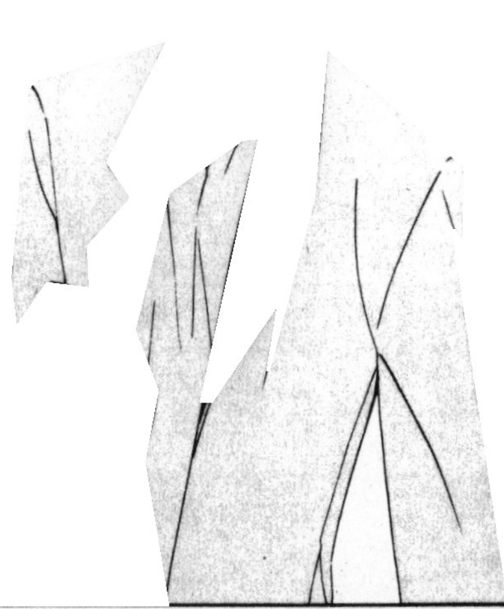
SHOULD I TELL YOU I'M SORRY FOR YOU?

I'M JEALOUS BECAUSE NO MATTER HOW IT ENDED...
...EVEN IF IT ONLY LASTED A MOMENT
...YOU GOT YOUR FEELINGS ACROSS.
IF I could just give up, would everythin be easier

But if I give up, my life is meaningless.

This love is the only proof that I'm alive.

The only thing flowing from my wounds is love.

I want her to understand that.

EVEN IF YOU GET YOUR FEELINGS ACROSS...

...THAT DOESN'T MEAN THAT THEY'LL ACCEPT YOU.

I want to scream it out loud.

THEY SAY YOU CAN'T MAKE PEOPLE FEEL WHAT YOU WANT THEM TO...

BUT I WONDER IF THAT'S TRUE.

ARE PEOPLE'S WILLS REALLY THAT STRONG?

I love her so much I don't know what to do with myself.

SHE COULD NEVER REFUSE LOVE...
...BECAUSE SHE'S A LONELY PERSON.
THAT'S WHERE I'M GOING TO GET IN.

THAT'S SCARY.
I THINK YOU REALLY MIGHT BE CRAZY.
BUT I'M DYING TO KNOW...
...JUST HOW YOUR ROMANCE TURNS OUT.
GRP
PLEASE GIVE ME A CALL...
...IF THE TWO OF YOU FALL IN LOVE.
THANKS FOR TODAY!
IT WAS FUN!
BYE!

He still believes that just getting his emotions across will make him happy.

Right now, I'm sure he couldn't understand...
...that ending things takes courage too.

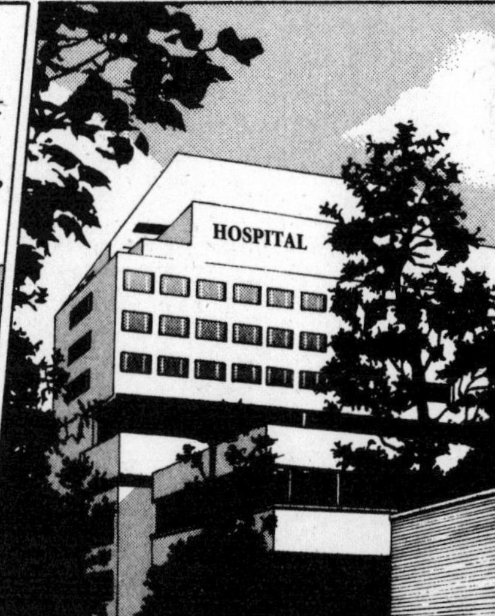

HOSPITAL

PINK ROSES. AND WILL YOU CUT OFF THE THORNS, PLEASE?
ARE YOU VISITING A FRIEND IN THE HOSPITAL?
NO. IT'S FOR A CELE-BRATION.
A NEW BABY...

BORN YESTER-DAY.
OH MY. CONGRAT-ULATIONS!

WAAAAAH
WAAAH

BYE-BYE.
WAAAH
BIG BROTH-ER.

HELLO!
CLICK
CON-GRAT-ULA-TIONS!
OH, KUMI!
KUMI-CHAN.

HE'S SO CUTE! SO YOU'RE MY NEPHEW, HUH?
THANK YOU.
YOU MUST BE TIRED, SIS.

I'M SURE HE'LL SURPASS MY BIG BROTHER...
...AND BECOME THE GREATEST GUY IN THE WORLD.

YOU KNOW ...
HISA-YOSHI, YOU REALLY ...
...DO NEED ME AROUND.
HMM ...

YOU WERE TALKING CRAZY.
KA TUNK
KA TUNK
MM...
YEAH, I KNOW.

THAT LADY SURE WAS WEIRD.
MM...
AND WE NEVER ASKED HER NAME.
Kumi♥
090.0000.XXXX
SHE TOLD ME.
HMM...

I WONDER IF THIS IS A COINCIDENCE...
...OR IF IT'S FATE?
KATUNK
KATUNK

But...

She and I are two different people...
...with two different loves.

I'M HOME!

I'M EX-HAUST-ED!
GEEZ ... YOU GOTTA HEAR WHAT HAP-PENED TODAY ...
MOM ?

Dear Rima,
Welcome home! I'm going out to dinner.
MAN ...
AT THIS HOUR? WHAT A DELINQUENT.
WHUMP
AAH ...
...
...
RINGALING
TIRED
OKAY ...
O-
OKAY ...

TAJIMA-KUN?
HI.
I WAS WONDERING HOW YOU WERE DOING.
YEAH, I'M FINE.
I WAS OUT TODAY.
HOW WAS SCHOOL?
WHAT?! YOU SKIPPED?

YOU SHOULD GO! WHAT A WASTE!
SORRY. YOU'RE RIGHT.
I'M SERIOUS!
HOW ARE YOU? THINGS GO ALL RIGHT TODAY?

I'M GLAD YOU CALLED, TAJIMA-KUN.
Since Mom's out...
LISTEN TO THIS...
YEAH.
IF I can talk to her even For a minute at the end of the day...
...the distance and the time we've been apart.

No one knows yet just how this love affair will end.

Lately...
I've been thinking a lot about how...
DING DONG

WHAT'S THAT?

THAT'S A WEIRD NOISE.

SOME-ONE'S RING-TONE?

OH.

THAT'S ME.

WHAT IS IT?

...getting used to things...

Hmm? ...

JOLT

DON'T YOU KNOW IT? IT'S "LUM'S LOVE SONG."

...isn't a good thing.

HELLO ?
WHAT, IKESHIBA-SAN?
I DON'T KNOW IT.
La la lalala!
I love Lum-chan.
I KNOW IT!
I LOVE THAT SHOW!
I WATCHED THE RERUNS.

STARE
BA-BMP
NAH ...
NEVER MIND ...

TMP
W-WELL THEN, I'LL BE GOING.
SEE YOU LATER!
TMP
BYE-BYE...
RIMA-CHAN.
BYE! ♥
OH.
HEY ...
TUNK
WAIT ...

I'LL GO WITH YOU.
WHY?
TA-JIMA-KUN.
WHY ARE YOU FOLLOWING ME?
BLUSH
EWW, DON'T COME WITH ME!
IT'S ON MY WAY.
I don't think it's good ...
IKESHIBA-SAN WANTS ME TO COME IN.
HE NEEDS YOU FOR SOMETHING?
I DON'T KNOW. HE SAID SOMETHING ABOUT A DEMO TAPE.
...to get too used to her being cold to me.
I get numb.
PAT
LET'S GO TOGETH-ER.

N-NO...
PUT YOURSELF IN THE SHOES OF THE ONE WHO'S BEING FOLLOWED ALL THE TIME.
I can't ...
...get used to her...
... hating me.
You don't love Tajima-kun, right?
OF...
OF course I don't!
Really?
I mean, I already love someone else.

Good.
To be honest...
Yurie-chan kind of annoys me.
More than Tajima-kun.
I find myself conscious of Yurie-chan.
So much...
So much...
And I get so incredibly...
...irritated.
...since she's decided I'm her rival.

Because she's wrong!
YOU'RE GOING TO THE STUDIO IN AOYAMA, RIGHT?
SORRY. HOW MUCH IS THE TICKET AGAIN?
IT'S OKAY. I'LL GET IT FROM IKESHIBA-SAN.
Why...
...have to look at me like that?
IT'S NOT LIKE WE DATING ANYTHI
WHY ARE YOU ALWAYS AROUND ME?
WANT ME TO HOLD YOUR BAG?
...does she...
I'D LIKE US TO BE DATING.

STOP IT. DON'T SAY STUFF LIKE THAT.
BLUSH
IT'S BECAUSE YOU'RE LIKE THAT THAT YURIE-CHAN...
GASP
THAT YURIE-CHAN?
DID SOMETHING HAPPEN?
NOTHING. NEVER MIND.
ANYWAY, I...
I AM NEVER EVER GOING TO FALL FOR YOU!
But if I wasn't numb...
...words...
...she doesn't even mean would hurt me.

THAT'S NOT...
...SOMETHING YOU CAN DECIDE FOR YOURSELF.
YOU CAN'T DECIDE ...
...WHOM YOU WILL OR WON'T FALL FOR!
Y—
YEAH— I CAN. THEY'RE MY FEEL- INGS!
BLUSH
AND I ALREADY LIKE SOMEONE ELSE!
YOU JUST DON'T GET IT!
YOU CAN'T SAY THAT!
I'M SICK OF THIS!

Why do I have to tiptoe around Yurie-chan?!
It's got nothing to do with me.
GOT IT.
THE NEXT TIME YOU TELL ME YOU HATE ME...
...I'LL TAKE IT SERIOUSLY.
I WON'T EVER FOLLOW YOU AROUND AGAIN.
THINK HARD BEFORE YOU SAY IT.

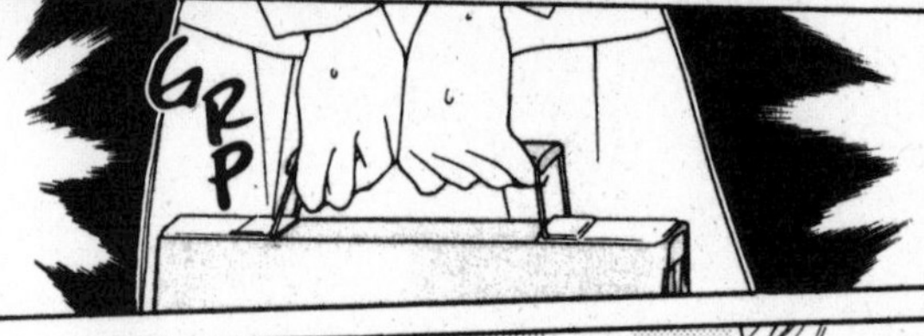
W-wait, what's that supposed to mean?
GRP
I'm always serious!

IF YOU DON'T WANT ME AROUND, YOU JUST HAVE TO SAY IT.
BUT DON'T SAY IT LIGHTLY IF YOU DON'T MEAN IT!

What the heck ?
He'll disappear if I tell him I hate him? I've been telling him that this whole time.

I mean, if I don't say that, it's like saying I... I like... like... like...
Like I like him or some-thing.
I can't have that!
I HATE YOU!

THE SHIBUYA TRAIN ON LINE FOUR...
...NOW ARRIV-ING...
...HEADING TO SUI-TENGU...
RRING
PLEASE STAY BEHIND THE WHITE LINE.

R
OKAY THEN.
I
DOORS ARE CLOSING.
N
G
GATUNK
W—
What the heck!

Idiot!
Tajima-kun is such an idiot!!
SHVR SHVR
I never led him on.
All of this was stuff Tajima-kun did completely on his own!
BUZZ BUZZ
From the very beginning I never once...
...said I liked him!
I basically dumped him just now, right?
UM ... ARE YOU ALL RIGHT?
So why do I feel like I'm the one who got dumped?
YES.
I'M FINE.

MORNING!

GOOD MORNING!

I'M SORRY I'M LATE!

RUSH

SWISH

GASP

TAJIMA-KUN.

WHY ARE YOU HERE?

FWIP

I CALLED HIM HERE.

He's ignoring me!

FUJIO-SAN, IT'S TIME FOR YOUR MAKEUP!

O— OKAY!

HURRY UP.

TAJIMA-KUN, YOU'LL BE HERE UNTIL RIMA-CHAN'S DONE, RIGHT?

LET'S ALL GO TO DINNER AFTER. I'LL CALL MANAMI-CHAN.

IKE-SHIBA-SAN.

I'LL BE HEADING HOME.

HUH?

MANAMI-CHAN'S DINNERS ARE ALWAYS SO GOOD...

SO I'LL BE EATING AT HOME.

HEH
YAHOO!
SULK
THAT MEANS WE'LL BE ALONE TOGETHER ON THE WAY HOME, RIGHT, IKESHIBA-SAN?
IS SOMETHING GOING ON WITH YOU TWO?
Y— YEAH.
WE'RE ACTING PERFECTLY NORMAL!
ALL RIGHT! I'M GONNA GO GET SOME WORK DONE!
Perfectly?
Oh!
DID SOMETHING HAPPEN?
HMM ... SO THEN SHE JUST TOLD YOU STRAIGHT OUT THAT SHE HATED YOU?
SQUEAK
YEAH ... SHE MADE IT VERY CLEAR.

Hmm...
THAT'S QUITE AN ADVANCED TECHNIQUE.
IT'S NOT A QUESTION OF TECH-NIQUE.
I MEANT IT.
THE ONLY THING I WANT IS REQUITED LOVE.
IF I CAN'T HAVE THAT, I DON'T NEED ANYTHING ELSE.
AFTER ALL...
...I'M NOT HER SLAVE.
AND HERE I WAS THINKING YOU WERE HER SLAVE.
YOU MAY NOT LIKE THE WORD "TECHNIQUE"...
BUT LOVE IS ALL ABOUT MANIPULATION. AND I THINK...

...WHAT YOU'RE DOING IS REALLY GOING TO SHAKE RIMA.

HEY, FUJIO-SAN!

YOU GOT A MINUTE?

GO AHEAD.

HEY, IT'S ABOUT TAJIMA-KUN. HE'S ON YOUR LABEL...

I DON'T KNOW MUCH ABOUT HIM.

I WAS WONDERING IF HE'S DATING ANYONE.

I HAVE NO IDEA.

WHY DON'T YOU ASK HIM?

I DID, AND HE SAID HE WASN'T.

BUT I THOUGHT I SHOULD DOUBLE-CHECK WITH YOU.

TWITCH

TUNK

IT'S GOT NOTHING TO DO WITH ME!

RIMA-CHAN ...

WHY'D YOU DRAG ME INTO IT?

WHAT'RE YOU DOING?

TA-JIMA-KUN.

KEEE

WHY ARE YOU STILL HERE?

GO HOME ALREADY!

GASP
E-
Ew...
He saw me looking like this...
Fore-head all ex-posed.

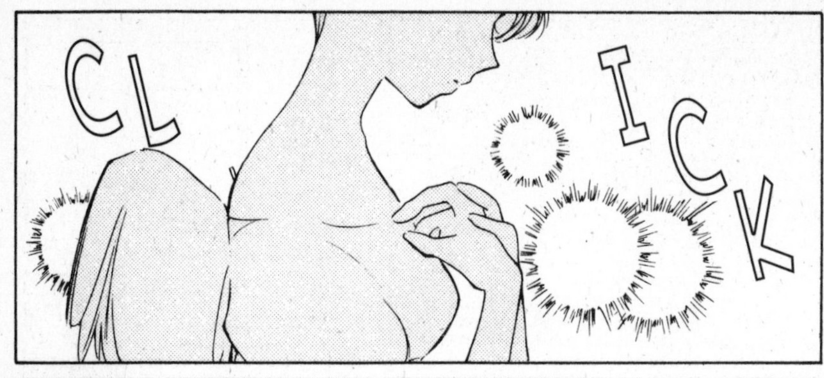
CLICK

OKAY, NOW LOOK OFF INTO THE DISTANCE ...
STARE
JUST MOVE AROUND FREELY.
RIMA-CHAN?
RIMA-CHAN?
WHAT'S UP?

EX—
EEEK!
EXCUSE ME! WHAT IS IT?
SEEMS LIKE YOU'RE HAVING TROUBLE CONCEN-TRATING. LET'S TAKE A BREAK.
A BREAK!
TAKE FIVE!

BLAH
EXCUSE ME.
I'M SORRY!

...
I WONDER IF SHE'S OKAY. SHE MUST BE TIRED.

SHE'S NOT THAT DELICATE.
THAT'S TRUE.
AND SHE'S FINALLY GOT THE LEAD ROLE IN A TV SHOW.

OH, WAS THAT FINALIZED?
FINALLY.
BLAH
WE FINALLY GOT AN INTERESTING STORYLINE.

THANKS FOR THE FOOD!
YOUR COOKING IS THE BEST, MANAMI-CHAN!

THANKS.
HEY, KUMI-CHAN...
HMM?
YOU'RE POPULAR AT SCHOOL, RIGHT?
NO, I'M NOT.
NO WAY. YOU'RE SO NICE TO GIRLS.
CLACK
I'LL DO THE WASHING UP.
I DON'T KNOW ...
KLAK
KLINK
...IF I'M THAT NICE.

WAIT, KUMI-CHAN...
SOMETHING HAPPENED, DIDN'T IT? TALK TO ME.
TELL ME ALL ABOUT IT, KUMI-CHAN.
YOUR FEELINGS FOR SOMEONE...
...OR YOUR PRIDE...
WHICH DO YOU THINK IS MORE IMPORTANT?

HUH? YOU MEAN ...
RIMA-CHAN WOUNDED YOUR PRIDE?!

IF YOU COULDN'T GET WHAT YOU WANTED, NO MATTER WHAT YOU DID...

COULD YOU MAKE DO WITH SOMETHING SIMILAR?

I COULD NEVER DO IT. I WANT WHAT I WANT.

WELL THEN, THANKS FOR ALL...

...YOUR HARD WORK TODAY.

THANK YOU!

I'LL GIVE YOU A RIDE HOME. GET IN.

THANK YOU!

IKE-SHIBA-SAN...

Hee hee hee

YOU'RE LIKE A PRINCE.

I THINK YOU MEAN AN OLD GEEZER.
WHAT?! THAT'S SO MEAN! YOU'RE NOT OLD!
I REALLY LOOK UP TO YOU.

YOU'RE DRUNK, RIMA-CHAN.
BOO
HEY, I'M NOT DRUNK!
YOU KNOW I ONLY HAD ONE GLASS OF BEER!
WHY DO YOU ALWAYS BRUSH ME OFF LIKE THAT?

I LIKE YOU.

CAN YOU STOP ...
... FOOLING AROUND ?!

OKAY, THEN ...
...CAN I KISS YOU?

BA BMP
HUH ?
BA BMP
BA BMP

THE LOVE YOU DON'T WANT ME TO BRUSH OFF...
IT MEANS DOING THINGS LIKE THAT, RIGHT ?

YOU DON'T KNOW ANYTHING ABOUT ME.
THAT'S NOT... TRUE.
I DO KNOW.
YOU DON'T KNOW THAT I REALLY DON'T LIKE VIRGINS, DO YOU?
W–
W–
W–
W–
W–
WHY NOT?
BECAUSE THEY'RE NO FUN.

He smells like cigarettes...
DIZZY
TREMBLE
THAT'S HOW GROWN-UPS KISS.

THAT'S FINE!
LET'S GO HOME THEN.
VROOOOM
I—
I'm not gonna cry!

CROWN OF LOVE VOL. 3 END

AFTERWORD

IT'S THE TIME OF YEAR WHEN FALL IS TURNING INTO WINTER.

Gargling is the most effective way to prevent catching a cold.

Let's use Lugol!*

To be continued in volume 4~

Yuki Kowaga 2000

* Lugol's iodine, a solution of elemental iodine and potassium iodide in water, is often used as a disinfectant or antiseptic.

CROWN OF LOVE

Vol. 3
Shojo Beat Edition

STORY & ART BY YUN KOUGA

Translation **HC Language Solutions, Inc.**
Touch-up Art & Lettering **Annaliese Christman**
Design **Frances O. Liddell**
Editor **Carrie Shepherd**

VP, Production **Alvin Lu**
VP, Sales & Product Marketing **Gonzalo Ferreyra**
VP, Creative **Linda Espinosa**
Publisher **Hyoe Narita**

Printed in the U.S.A.

Published by VIZ Media, LLC
P.O. Box 77010
San Francisco, CA 94107

10 9 8 7 6 5 4 3 2 1
First printing, August 2010